T0146362

Disruption Without Change

The Consequences of COVID-19 on the Global
Economic Balance

HOWARD J. SHATZ

Prepared for the Department of the Air Force
Approved for public release; distribution unlimited

 PROJECT AIR FORCE

For more information on this publication, visit **www.rand.org/t/RRA1464-1**.

About RAND

The RAND Corporation is a research organization that develops solutions to public policy challenges to help make communities throughout the world safer and more secure, healthier and more prosperous. RAND is nonprofit, nonpartisan, and committed to the public interest. To learn more about RAND, visit www.rand.org.

Research Integrity

Our mission to help improve policy and decisionmaking through research and analysis is enabled through our core values of quality and objectivity and our unwavering commitment to the highest level of integrity and ethical behavior. To help ensure our research and analysis are rigorous, objective, and nonpartisan, we subject our research publications to a robust and exacting quality-assurance process; avoid both the appearance and reality of financial and other conflicts of interest through staff training, project screening, and a policy of mandatory disclosure; and pursue transparency in our research engagements through our commitment to the open publication of our research findings and recommendations, disclosure of the source of funding of published research, and policies to ensure intellectual independence. For more information, visit www.rand.org/about/principles.

About This Report

The coronavirus disease 2019 pandemic has upended the global economy, resulting in large losses of gross domestic product worldwide. This report reviews the economic track record of the United States and its main competitors and allies to discern how the dramatic economic changes induced by the disease could affect geopolitical competition and the future security environment. The report uses data through August 31, 2021. This research was completed in September 2021, before the February 2022 Russian invasion of Ukraine. It has not been subsequently revised.

The research reported here was conducted within the Strategy and Doctrine Program of RAND Project AIR FORCE as part of fiscal year 2021 concept formulation.

The views expressed in this report are those of the author and do not reflect the official policy or position of the United States Air Force, the Department of Defense, or the U.S. government.

RAND Project AIR FORCE

RAND Project AIR FORCE (PAF), a division of the RAND Corporation, is the Department of the Air Force's (DAF's) federally funded research and development center for studies and analyses, supporting both the United States Air Force and the United States Space Force. PAF provides the DAF with independent analyses of policy alternatives affecting the development, employment, combat readiness, and support of current and future air, space, and cyber forces. Research is conducted in four programs: Strategy and Doctrine; Force Modernization and Employment; Resource Management; and Workforce, Development, and Health. The research reported here was prepared under contract FA7014-16-D-1000.

Additional information about PAF is available on our website: www.rand.org/paf/

The draft report, issued on June 14, 2021, was reviewed by formal peer reviewers and DAF subject-matter experts.

Funding

Funding for this research was made possible through the concept formulation provision of the Department of the Air Force–RAND Sponsoring Agreement. PAF uses concept formulation funding to support a variety of activities, including research plan development; direct assistance on short-term, decision-focused Department of the Air Force requests; exploratory research; outreach and communications initiatives; and other efforts undertaken in support of the development, execution, management, and reporting of PAF's approved research agenda.

Acknowledgments

I thank Raphael Cohen of the RAND Corporation for conceiving of and supporting this report and James Dobbins and Krishna Kumar of RAND, as well as Thomas Wright of the Brookings Institution, for thoughtful reviews that greatly improved the report's quality. At RAND, Julienne Ackerman managed the production of this report, Katie Hynes provided expert copy editing, and Sandy Petitjean prepared the figure art. All errors of fact and interpretation remain my responsibility.

Summary

The coronavirus disease 2019 (COVID-19) pandemic caused the largest drop in global economic activity since World War II and has the potential to disrupt international relations in ways that were still developing as of the conclusion of this research in late summer 2021. As of January 31, 2020, there were fewer than 10,000 confirmed cases worldwide. By August 31, 2021, there were more than 217.71 million confirmed cases and 4.52 million confirmed deaths, according to data tracked by *Our World in Data.*

But by the time the pandemic was well into its second year, an unexpected pattern had emerged. Although the world's worst pandemic in a century might have accelerated previous trends, it had not changed much about the international economic order. China was the only major economy to show positive economic growth in 2020 relative to 2019 but reversed necessary domestic reforms to do so. The United States was the best-performing advanced Western economy in 2020 but greatly increased its federal debt. Europe and U.S. treaty allies performed less well. Prepandemic trends persisted: China's share of the global economy was growing, that of the United States was holding steady, and that of U.S. allies was declining.

Approach

This report provides a review of economic developments in the United States; major U.S. competitors China and Russia; and U.S. allies and partners, including the European Union (EU), the United Kingdom (UK), Japan, Australia, and India. It focuses on the global economic balance, or *geoeconomic balance*—that is, the relative size and influence of national economies in the global economy. The report also discusses what has come to be known as *vaccine diplomacy,* or the effort to distribute vaccines to developing countries, which is exemplary of how the pandemic has affected global competition. It draws on official data releases, reports by international organizations, and media reports and uses data released through August 31, 2021. This research was completed in September 2021, before the February 2022 Russian invasion of Ukraine. It has not been subsequently revised.

Key Findings

Economic performance extended existing trends and exacerbated existing problems such that the geoeconomic balance had not changed as of late summer 2021. The pandemic also opened up a new field of global competition: vaccine diplomacy.

- The United States performed better than other major advanced economies, helped by several major stimulus bills. Continued plans for additional high spending levels have raised concerns about inflation and debt. In addition, the pandemic exacerbated inequality.
- China was the only major economy to experience positive economic growth in 2020. However, this came at the cost of a reversal of China's economic reform attempts, with debt relative to gross domestic product (GDP) rising. Russia's economy declined less than expected, but the decline was still large. With oil prices rising in 2021, Russia's recovery appears to be on track.
- Among U.S. allies and partners, the EU performed poorly in 2020 and then had a further GDP decline in the first quarter of 2021. The UK was the worst-performing major advanced economy. As in most other countries, Japan's GDP fell in 2020, and partly because of a COVID-19 resurgence, it fell in the first quarter of 2021. Australia performed relatively better than most advanced economies. India had a steep decline in 2020, and although it was thought to have COVID-19 under control in late 2020, the disease surged in the spring of 2021.
- Leaving the populations of lower-income countries unvaccinated presents a variety of risks. Most prominently, new variants could develop, endangering the world. As well, these countries will continue to suffer economically, slowing the global recovery.
- COVID-19 opened a new field of global competition: distributing vaccines to low- and middle-income countries to claim credit for being a responsible provider of global public goods.

Implications for Policymakers and Defense Planners

From an economic and social standpoint, COVID-19 upended the world, but its effect on the global balance of power has so far proved modest.

- The success of Operation Warp Speed, the U.S. effort that brought the vaccine to market, could make U.S. policymakers across the political spectrum more open to industrial policy and government intervention in the economy. Although the effort could be viewed as equivalent to a wartime measure in which results were more important than cost and perhaps not applicable to normal times, the model could be adapted for the future.
- Likewise, new fiscal measures by the EU could stabilize growth on the continent and make the euro a larger factor among reserve currencies.
- The pandemic showed that global competition has wide bounds and now includes promises to safeguard the world's health. Vaccine diplomacy became an ongoing activity, but one for which it is too early yet to conclude which countries will benefit.
- China continued to grow economically and modernize its armed forces. Russia's economy declined, but most of the country's defense activities have relatively modest cost. Accordingly, at least as of mid-2021, the pandemic did not call for major changes in the U.S. stance toward major competitors.
- However, the extent to which U.S. allies will increase their contributions to collective defense efforts is a continuing issue heightened by lower levels of growth in Europe. And ambitious plans for federal spending and investment in the United States for civilian purposes might mean additional pressure on the U.S. defense budget, although the fiscal year 2022 budget proposal still plans for a small defense spending increase.
- The international response to this global pandemic exposed a gap in U.S. leadership, which is only beginning to be redressed.

There are also a variety of risks and uncertainties that could affect the global geoeconomic balance. Among these are the evolution of globalization; damage to and resilience of international cooperation; and the consequences of the pandemic for national cohesion, support for government, and trust in expertise, which has been reduced.

Contents

CHAPTER ONE

The COVID-19 Disruption

The coronavirus disease 2019 (COVID-19) pandemic disrupted the global economy and international relations in ways that are still developing. As of January 31, 2020, there were fewer than 10,000 confirmed cases worldwide. By August 31, 2021, there were more than 217.71 million confirmed cases and 4.52 million confirmed deaths.[1] The number of cases is likely an undercount because of limited testing, although there is uncertainty around the number of deaths because of both limited testing and challenges in attribution. For example, one analysis estimates that the number of cases in China in January 2020 was actually 37 times higher than the number reported.[2]

The uncertain course of the disease also meant an uncertain understanding of how the pandemic might affect the global economy and geopolitical relations. Once it was recognized that a global pandemic was emerging, it was clear that this would deliver a widespread negative economic shock. What was less clear was how different countries would be affected. Countries whose economies emerged more quickly would find themselves having greater weight in the global economy, with the potential to more strongly influence its evolution and its future governance. Early analysis speculated

---

[1] Our World in Data, "COVID-19 Data Explorer," webpage, undated; data accessed September 1, 2021.

[2] Christopher A. Mouton, Russell Hanson, Adam R. Grissom, and John P. Godges, *COVID-19 Air Traffic Visualization: COVID-19 Cases in China Were Likely 37 Times Higher than Reported in January 2020*, Santa Monica, Calif.: RAND Corporation, RR-A248-3, 2020.

on possible alterations to the global order and steps that might help position the United States and its allies favorably.[3]

A World Reordered?

But by the time the pandemic was well into its second year, an unexpected pattern had emerged. Although the world's worst pandemic in a century might have accelerated previous geopolitical trends—and even that outcome might be doubtful—it had not changed the international order much. Any fears that it could have floored the United States, devastated Russia, and boosted China into global ascendancy had not materialized, at least as of summer 2021. It is true that China emerged as the only major economy to show positive growth in annual gross domestic product (GDP) in 2020 relative to 2019. But the United States was the best-performing advanced Western economy in 2020 despite its checkered record of containing the disease.

Some countries did lose out badly. The United States' European and North Atlantic Treaty Organization (NATO) allies performed poorly as a group, but this only marginally affected prepandemic trends in which China's share of the global economy was growing, that of the United States was holding steady, and that of U.S. allies was declining.[4] Some other trends reversed. The most notable trend reversal was that of India, which had appeared to get the virus under control only to see it come roaring back in early 2021. But overall, the pandemic had accelerated ongoing trends but did not introduce any major breaks in geopolitical competition. For the United States, the biggest consequence might be that as geopolitical competition continues, allies and partners will be weaker than U.S. leaders had hoped, putting more of a burden on the United States to maintain and advance the

---

[3] See, for example, Robert D. Blackwill and Thomas Wright, "Why COVID-19 Presents a World Reordering Moment," *National Interest*, July 11, 2020; Daniel Twining and Patrick Quirk, "Winning the Great Power Competition Post-Pandemic," *American Interest*, May 11, 2020; Kurt M. Campbell and Rush Doshi, "The Coronavirus Could Reshape Global Order," *Foreign Affairs*, March 18, 2020.

[4] Howard J. Shatz and Nathan Chandler, *Global Economic Trends and the Future of Warfare: The Changing Global Environment and Its Implications for the U.S. Air Force*, Santa Monica, Calif.: RAND Corporation, RR-2849/4-AF, 2020.

Western-oriented, rules-based international order that has benefited populations globally since the end of World War II.

The Plan for This Report

This report reviews two topics. First, it looks at the global economic balance—*the geoeconomic balance*—as represented by national economic performance and exemplified by changes in GDP but including other measures where useful in countries and regions that are consequential for the global economic balance, specifically the United States, U.S. competitors China and Russia, U.S. allies and partners, and the developing world as a whole.[5] The term *geoeconomic balance* is meant to signify the relative size and influence of national economies in the global economy and the trends in size and influence. The report considers geoeconomic balance by drawing on official data as provided by each country and data provided by multilateral institutions.[6] Certainly, other COVID-19 outcomes, such as hospitalizations and deaths, have economic consequences, but these will be encapsulated in GDP. Likewise, GDP might not capture other economic phenomena, such as employment, but it can serve as a good shorthand for overall economic performance. More directly related to geopolitical competition, the size of an economy in terms of GDP is foundational to its ability to supply public goods and government services and maintain a global diplomatic service and a strong defense. The report includes vaccination rates because vaccinations have helped tamp down the disease, which in turn has enabled economies to reopen more fully.

---

[5] With this focus, the report omits a specific discussion of Iran and North Korea, two countries that are consequential for U.S. national security planning but not for the global economic balance.

[6] GDP provides a quick take on economic performance, but there is more to consider, including unemployment and increased government debt. Beyond these economic indicators, there are social indicators that are likely to have long-term consequences, such as gaps in education that include learning loss from moving classes from in-person to online or simply shutting down schools (Per Engzell, Arun Frey, and Mark D. Verhagen, "Learning Loss Due to School Closures During the COVID-19 Pandemic," *PNAS*, Vol. 118, No. 17, 2021).

Second, the report focuses on one form of global competition that has emerged with the pandemic: *vaccine diplomacy*, or the race to provide COVID-19 vaccines to lower- and middle-income countries that can neither create their own nor afford to purchase supplies from the market. Vaccine diplomacy is relevant for several reasons. First, from a geopolitical competition perspective, it shows the ways that competition can fill unoccupied spaces and is not just about political and economic systems. Second, ensuring vaccines worldwide is an important way to make sure the pandemic is controlled, given the risks of mutations occurring and spread by travel. Furthermore, countries hurt by the pandemic will underperform economically, hurting global trade and exacerbating global poverty. Finally, ensuring vaccine supplies accords with the ethos of the international system to ensure that the benefits of scientific discovery and economic development are widespread.[7]

A review of the economic record and efforts to supply vaccines is followed by a final chapter, which notes other economic consequences that merit further investigation in future work and discusses policy implications for the U.S. government and the U.S. defense establishment. These implications might be relevant to allies and partners as well.[8]

There is one important caveat to the findings in this report. This report uses data available through August 31, 2021. As of the time of writing, August 2021, the global situation regarding COVID-19 and its variants remained fluid; there had been outbreaks emerging throughout the world and returns to mitigation measures in some jurisdictions that had loosened them. In early July 2021, because the delta variant had already been found in 85 countries, many governments in Asia and Europe had reintroduced

---

[7] For more on the many benefits of ensuring widespread distribution and use of vaccines, see Krishna Kumar, "Why America Must Do More to Vaccinate the World's Population," *National Interest*, May 3, 2021a.

[8] The pandemic has had many more implications for the world than just the geoeconomic balance and the race to provide vaccines. For one look at the effects of COVID-19 on the international order, see Colin Kahl and Thomas Wright, *Aftershocks: Pandemic Politics and the End of the Old International Order*, New York: St. Martin's Press, 2021.

travel restrictions and delayed the end of lockdowns.[9] But at the same time, the economic trends that had emerged in late 2020 and early 2021 were largely intact, suggesting that even with an evolving pandemic, people, businesses, and governments were adjusting in a way that would allow them to return to a more normal level of economic activity.[10]

---

[9] Paul Hannon, Gabriele Steinhauser, and Sha Hua, "Delta Variant's Spread Hobbles Global Efforts to Lift Covid-19 Restrictions," *Wall Street Journal*, July 1, 2021.

[10] This research was completed in September 2021, before the February 2022 Russian invasion of Ukraine. It has not been subsequently revised.

CHAPTER TWO

The Economic Outcomes

The emergence of the pandemic introduced great uncertainty into international economic affairs. But in the end, the global economy and that of many countries performed better than the worst expectations.

Annual Gross Domestic Product Outcomes

One way to understand this uncertainty is to review the economic projections of the change in 2020 GDP relative to 2019 GDP published by the International Monetary Fund (IMF) in its *World Economic Outlook* series (Figure 2.1). These projections make clear that the effects of the pandemic were difficult to predict.

In January 2020, even after cases had started to arise in Wuhan, a city in Hubei Province, China, the IMF projected that global growth in 2020 would be 3.3 percent. However, by April 2020, it was clear that the pandemic would have more-dramatic negative consequences, and the IMF revised its projection downward by 6.3 percentage points to –3.0 percent. During the spring, it appeared that the course of the pandemic would be even worse than expected, and the IMF revised its projection further downward in June 2020 to –4.9 percent (shown in Figure 2.1). This downward projection applied to every major economy. During the summer, trends began to improve and economies began to adjust, and in October 2020 the IMF revised its projections upward, although nearly all projections remained deeply negative.

In the end, as shown by the "April 2021 actual" bars in the figure, most countries—but not all—did better than the worst expectations. With most countries reporting at least preliminary data for all of 2020, the outcome of –3.3 percent for the world is somewhat worse than initially expected in

FIGURE 2.1

Economic Growth for 2020 Relative to 2019

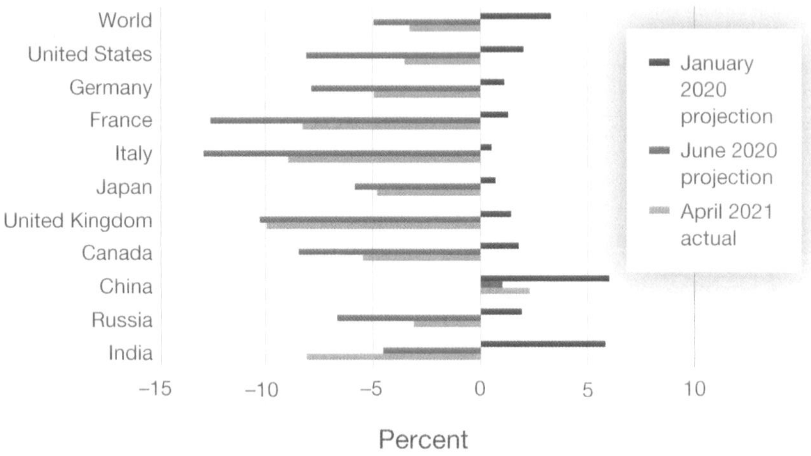

SOURCE: IMF, *World Economic Outlook: Managing Divergent Recoveries*, Washington, D.C., April 2021b; IMF, *World Economic Outlook Update: A Crisis Like No Other, an Uncertain Recovery*, Washington, D.C., June 2020b; IMF, *World Economic Outlook Update: An Update of the Key WEO Projections*, Washington, D.C., January 20, 2020a.

NOTE: Figures published in April 2021 are actual outcomes but are subject to revision and might be slightly different from those reported by national sources. Economically advanced economies generally experience slower growth while emerging economies, such as China and India, usually are able to grow faster because they are able to use advanced-country technology and access advanced-country markets to help them catch up. This partly explains why the January 2020 projections for China, India, and the world (constituted mostly by developed and emerging economies) are above those for the economically advanced countries.

April 2020 (–3.0 percent) but better than expected in June 2020 (–4.9 percent). The United States fared much better than expected, as did Russia and China. Europe was mixed, but no major European countries performed more strongly than the United States.

Quarterly Gross Domestic Product Outcomes

Just as the projections were at their worst in midyear, so was actual economic performance. By midyear, and especially in the April 2020 to June 2020 period, most countries were badly affected. One way to see this is to consider the change in GDP in a specific quarter of one year relative to GDP in the same quarter the year before (Figure 2.2). Given some of the growth disparities, it is easy to see why one might imagine a world reordered.

In the United States, GDP in the second quarter of 2020 was 9 percent below that in the second quarter of 2019, and that was one of the milder declines. The European Union (EU)—especially the south—and the United Kingdom (UK) had the largest declines of the major economies, and double-digit declines were common throughout the EU. The Group of Seven (G-7) economies of Japan and Canada also experienced a double-digit decline in the second quarter. China experienced its major COVID-19 decline earlier, in the first quarter, when GDP fell 6.8 percent—the first quarterly decline since China started reporting its quarterly GDP in 1992. Considering that China's quarterly GDP was regularly in the range of positive 6 percent, this represented a decline on par with that of the other, slower-growing major economies.

Most economies started to recover by the third quarter. By the end of 2020, many economies were experiencing positive growth once again as measured by fourth quarter GDP relative to third quarter GDP (not shown in the figure). Among the G-7 countries, only France and Italy continued to experience an economic decline. However, no major Western country ended 2020 with GDP higher than the level at the end of 2019, as measured by the change from the fourth quarter of 2019 to the fourth quarter of 2020 (the second bar for each country or country group in Figure 2.2). U.S. GDP at the end of 2020 was 2.4 percent below GDP at the end of 2019, GDP in the 27 countries of the EU was 4.6 percent lower, and UK GDP was 7.3 percent lower, the worst of all major economies. Only China ended the year with GDP higher than it started at the beginning of the year.

Continued Uncertainty into 2021

The 2020 downturn resulted in a loss of more than $5 trillion worth of global GDP when valued at 2010 U.S. dollars—more than the annual GDP of every individual country in the world except the United States, China,

FIGURE 2.2

The Gross Domestic Product Growth Collapse and Restoration

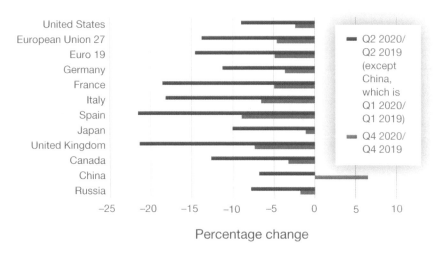

Percentage change

SOURCE: U.S. Bureau of Economic Analysis, "Gross Domestic Product (Third Estimate), GDP by Industry, and Corporate Profits, Fourth Quarter and Year 2020," news release, Suitland, Md., BEA 21–11, March 25, 2021b; U.S. Bureau of Economic Analysis, "Current-Dollar and 'Real' Gross Domestic Product," Excel spreadsheet gdplev.xlsx, March 25, 2021a; Eurostat, "GDP and Main Components (Output, Expenditure and Income) [NAMA_10_GDP$DEFAULTVIEW]," spreadsheet from online database, last updated April 1, 2021a; Eurostat, "GDP and Main Components (Output, Expenditure and Income) [NAMQ_10_GDP$DEFAULTVIEW]," spreadsheet from online database, last updated April 1, 2021b; Office for National Statistics (United Kingdom), "GDP Quarterly National Accounts, UK: October to December 2020," statistical bulletin, March 31, 2021a; Economic and Social Research Office, Cabinet Office, Government of Japan, "Quarterly Estimates of GDP: January–March 2021 (1st Preliminary)," May 18, 2021a; Statistics Canada, "Gross Domestic Product, Income and Expenditure, Fourth Quarter 2020," The Daily, March 2, 2021a; Statistics Canada, Table 36-10-0104-01 Gross Domestic Product, Expenditure-Based, Canada, Quarterly (x 1,000,000)," downloaded April 2, 2021b; National Bureau of Statistics of China, "Preliminary Accounting Results of GDP for the Fourth Quarter and the Whole Year of 2020," press release, Beijing, January 20, 2021a; National Bureau of Statistics of China, "National Economy Made a Good Start in the First Quarter," press release, Beijing, April 16, 2021c; Federal State Statistical Service (Rosstat), "Rosstat Presents the Second GDP Estimate for 2020" ["Росстат представил вторую оценку ВВП за 2020 год"], News of Rosstat, April 1, 2021c; Federal State Statistical Service (Rosstat), "Production and Use of Gross Domestic Product (GDP) for 2020" ["О производстве и использовании валового внутреннего продукта (ВВП) за 2020 год"], April 1, 2021b; Federal State Statistical Service (Rosstat), "Gross Domestic Product (at 2016 Prices, Bln Rubles)" ["Валовой нутрений продукт (в ценах 2016г., млрд.руб.)"], Tab 6b, spreadsheet, last updated April 1, 2021a.

NOTE: Q2 = second quarter; Q4 = fourth quarter. Figures for the worst quarter are for the quarter in 2020 relative to the quarter in 2019. For all but China, this is the second quarter of 2020; for China, it is the first quarter of 2020. Countries also report quarterly growth relative to the immediate past quarter. Measured this way, the worst quarter remains the same for each economy, but the numbers are different. European Union 27 includes aggregate data for all 27 members of the European Union. Euro 19 includes aggregate data for the 19 members of the European Union that have adopted the euro as their national currency.

and Japan.[1] Although most economies had started to grow, several experienced economic setbacks in 2021, as discussed in subsequent chapters. In addition, even though it appeared that the pandemic was receding in early 2021, by late spring 2021, COVID-19 had not only resurged and reached dire levels in India but also reappeared in parts of Asia that had seemed to have defeated it.[2] This led to new restrictions that had economic implications.

One reason the global economy ended up doing better than expected was that countries around the world rolled out sizable stimulus measures to either maintain employment or help people who lost their jobs. The downturn could have been far worse otherwise. However, these measures have the potential to cause future problems. Given the uncertain course of the disease, the potential for new variants, and the need to finance the deficits run up by the economic rescue plans, the conclusions reached in this report cannot be taken as final. Economic and disease patterns must be monitored. But even with this uncertainty, the evidence so far weighs against assuming that global patterns of relative economic performance will change dramatically.

---

[1] The World Bank's *World Development Indicators* database provides a figure of slightly more than $84.8 trillion for world GDP in 2019 as measured in 2010 U.S. dollars. Had the world economy grown as expected, GDP would have been almost $87.4 trillion. However, with a 3.3 percent decline, estimated real GDP in 2020 would have been $82 trillion. The world GDP variable is "GDP (constant 2010 US$)," NY.GDP.MKTP. KD, with data as of April 26, 2021 (World Bank Group, *World Development Indicators*, database, Washington, D.C., version last updated October 15, 2020).

[2] Niharika Mandhana, "Asia Suffers Outbreaks Where COVID-19 Had Seemed Beaten," *Wall Street Journal*, May 19, 2021.

CHAPTER THREE

COVID-19 and the United States

Beset throughout 2020 by heightened levels of political polarization, domestic unrest, uneven performance in dealing with the public health emergency, and a high rate of COVID-19 cases and deaths relative to the population, the United States performed better than expected economically during the pandemic.[1] It fielded a major vaccine drive well ahead of most other advanced economies. With this record and sizable continued stimulus spending by the federal government, it was expected that the United States would not only continue to grow strongly in 2021 but also drive growth worldwide. In its July 2021 outlook, the IMF projected that the U.S. economy would grow 5.6 percent in 2021, an increase from the 4.9 percent projection in its April 2021 outlook.[2]

The U.S. Economy in 2020 and 2021

The IMF initially projected that the U.S. economy would decline by 5.9 percent in 2020 and then lowered that projection even further to –8.0 percent in its June 2020 projection (Figure 2.1). However, the economy finished the year down 3.5 percent relative to 2019. By the first quarter of 2021, real seasonally adjusted GDP was down less than 1 percent from its peak in the

---

[1] Riots, vandalism, and looting from May 26, 2020, to June 8, 2020, following the death of George Floyd in Minneapolis police custody are reported to have caused losses of between $1 billion and $2 billion to the insurance industry. This makes these civil unrest events the costliest in the United States to the insurance industry since at least 1950 (Jennifer A. Kingson, "Exclusive: $1 Billion-Plus Riot Damage Is Most Expensive in Insurance History," *Axios*, September 16, 2020).

[2] IMF, 2021b, p. 6.

fourth quarter of 2019, and by the second quarter of 2021, it had hit an all-time high of almost $19.4 trillion on an annualized basis in chained 2012 U.S. dollars.[3]

The U.S. decline started in the first three months of 2020, when GDP fell by 1.3 percent. It then fell by 8.9 percent, the largest quarterly drop since World War II, and then in the third quarter it rose by 7.5 percent, the largest quarterly increase since World War II. GDP continued growing, rising by 1.1 percent in the last quarter of 2020 and then by 1.5 percent in the first quarter and 1.6 percent in the second quarter of 2021.[4]

Fiscal Stimulus for Fiscal Year 2020

The United States instituted considerable fiscal stimulus in 2020 to maintain economic activity, passing four bills in March and April 2020, which together were to inject $2.2 trillion into the U.S. economy in 2020, or about 10 percent of U.S. GDP.[5] The centerpiece of this was the bipartisan Coronavirus Aid, Relief, and Economic Security Act, signed by President Donald J. Trump in late March 2020, early in the pandemic. It was expected to inject $1.6 trillion into the economy through September 2020—or 7.4 percent of nominal GDP as measured in the first quarter of 2020—with a combination of extra spending and tax credits, and then an additional $448 billion

---

[3] Second quarter 2021 GDP totaled $19.358 trillion (advance estimate), first quarter 2021 GDP totaled $19.056 trillion, and fourth quarter 2019 GDP totaled $19.202 trillion (U.S. Bureau of Economic Analysis, "Current-Dollar and 'Real' Gross Domestic Product," Excel spreadsheet gdplev.xlsx, July 29, 2021e).

[4] The United States usually annualizes quarterly GDP growth rates, so the second quarter 2020 GDP decline was announced as –31.2 percent, the third quarter 2020 GDP increase was announced as 33.8 percent, the first quarter 2021 GDP increase was announced as 6.3 percent, and the second quarter 2021 GDP increase was announced as 6.5 percent for the advance estimate (U.S. Bureau of Economic Analysis, "Gross Domestic Product, Second Quarter 2021 (Advance Estimate) and Annual Update," BEA 21–36, July 29, 2021f). Most other countries do not annualize, so to keep the reporting consistent across countries, this report generally does not annualize U.S. growth rates in the main text.

[5] Theresa Gullo, "Estimating the Federal Budgetary Effects of Pandemic-Related Legislation: A Presentation to the Association for Budgeting and Financial Management's 2020 Virtual Symposium," slide deck, Congressional Budget Office, September 25, 2020.

through September 2021. It also authorized up to $454 billion for emergency lending by the Federal Reserve.[6] Although two of the other laws had much smaller amounts, the other piece of major legislation was the Paycheck Protection Program and Health Care Enhancement Act, signed into law on April 24, 2020, and projected to inject $434 billion into the economy through September 30, 2020, and an additional $42.7 billion through September 30, 2021.[7]

Fiscal Stimulus for Fiscal Year 2021

Even after that major legislation, stimulus continued. Members of Congress attempted new bills throughout the year but could not agree. Finally, in the Consolidated Appropriations Act, signed December 27, 2020, Congress included measures to inject an additional $737 billion through September 30, 2021, and $74 billion through September 30, 2022.[8]

When the Joe Biden administration took office in January 2021, the U.S. economy was still not back to where it had been before the pandemic. U.S. nonfarm employment peaked at 152.5 million in February 2020 and then collapsed to 130.2 million in April 2020 before it started rebounding the next month. By October 2020, it hit 142.5 million but then stayed in the range of 142.5 to 142.8 million through January 2021.[9]

---

[6] Phillip L. Swagel, Director, U.S. Congressional Budget Office, "Preliminary Estimate of the Effects of H.R. 748, the CARES Act, Public Law 116-136, Revised, with Corrections to the Revenue Effect of the Employee Retention Credit and to the Modification of a Limitation on Losses for Taxpayers Other Than Corporations," analysis to Honorable Mike Enzi, Chairman, Committee on the Budget, U.S. Senate, revised April 27, 2020.

[7] U.S. Congressional Budget Office, "CBO Estimate for H.R. 266, the Paycheck Protection Program and Health Care Enhancement Act as Passed by the Senate on April 21, 2020," April 22, 2020.

[8] U.S. Congressional Budget Office, "Summary Estimate for Divisions M Through FF, H.R. 133, Consolidated Appropriations Act, 2021, Public Law 116-260, Enacted on December 27, 2020," January 14, 2021a. Additional, declining amounts were to be spent in later years as well.

[9] U.S. Bureau of Labor Statistics, "All Employees, Thousands, Total Nonfarm, Seasonally Adjusted," Series ID CES0000000001, Employment, Hours, and Earnings from the Current Employment Statistics Survey (National), online data, extracted May 25, 2021, and September 5, 2021.

Building on previous stimulus bills, Congress passed and the Biden administration enacted the American Rescue Plan on March 11, 2021. This bill was estimated to have $1.16 trillion in spending and tax relief (nearly all of which is new spending) through September 30, 2021, and then an additional $528.5 billion through September 30, 2022, and $114.3 billion through September 30, 2023.[10] The 2021 spending in the Consolidated Appropriations Act and the American Rescue Plan together amount to $1.9 trillion, or 8.6 percent of U.S. nominal GDP as registered in the first quarter of calendar year 2021.

Monetary Stimulus

In March 2020, during the early days of the pandemic, the Federal Reserve announced several facilities to restore liquidity to financial markets, starting with the purchase of Treasury securities.[11] At the same time, the federal government embarked on its fiscal stimulus programs. Over the next several months, federal debt rose dramatically, and almost all of this was effectively monetized through Federal Reserve purchases. In March 2020, federal debt held by the public daily averaged $17.5 trillion, rising from $17.4 trillion to $17.7 trillion. By June 4, 2020, the same figure hit $20.0 trillion but then continued a much slower increase, hitting almost $22.3 trillion on August 31, 2021.[12]

Focusing on dates comparable to U.S. Federal Reserve reporting shows that federal debt issued by the U.S. Treasury increased by $2.464 trillion between March 11, 2020, and June 3, 2020. Between those same dates, U.S. Treasury securities on the Federal Reserve balance sheet rose from $2.5 tril-

---

[10] U.S. Congressional Budget Office, "Estimated Budgetary Effects of H.R. 1319, American Rescue Plan Act of 2021, as Passed by the Senate on March 6, 2021," cost estimate, March 10, 2021d.

[11] Federal Reserve Bank of New York, "Statement Regarding Treasury Reserve Management Purchases and Repurchase Operations," March 12, 2020. Numerous additional Federal Reserve actions were announced later in March 2020 (Board of Governors of the Federal Reserve System, "Federal Reserve Announces Extensive New Measures to Support the Economy," press release, Washington, D.C., March 23, 2020a).

[12] U.S. Department of the Treasury, "Debt to the Penny," online database, undated a.

lion to $4.1 trillion, a gain of $1.611 trillion, or 65 percent of total new federal debt issued.[13]

Effects of the Stimulus and Concerns

The Consolidated Appropriations Act and especially the American Rescue Plan are expected to spur U.S. economic activity considerably, but they are also expected to serve as a stimulus to the rest of the world.[14] One analysis suggested that the new stimulus would raise U.S. GDP growth for 2021 to 5.3 percent relative to 2020 and increase imports of goods and services by $270 billion in 2021—about 11 percent of 2020 imports of goods and services—and an additional $90 billion in 2022.[15]

As of the writing of this report, more large-scale spending was under discussion. In August 2021, the Senate approved a bipartisan infrastructure bill that provided for $782.5 billion in contract authority between fiscal years 2022 (starting October 1, 2021) and 2031.[16] In addition, the administration proposed a $6 trillion budget for fiscal year 2022 that included a proposed deficit of $1.8 trillion and a rise in annual spending to $8.2 trillion by 2031.[17] Federal spending hit record highs of $4.1 trillion in fiscal year 2018 and $4.4 trillion in fiscal year 2019, and then it jumped to almost $6.6 trillion in fiscal year 2020, the pandemic year, and was expected to decline to

---

[13] Board of Governors of the Federal Reserve System, "Factors Affecting Reserve Balances," statistical release, H.4.1, May 27, 2021b. Data were downloaded May 28, 2021, from the online data download program data facility (Board of Governors of the Federal Reserve System, "Factors Affecting Reserve Balances," statistical release data download program, H.4.1, May 27, 2021c). See also Board of Governors of the Federal Reserve System, "Credit and Liquidity Programs and Balance Sheet," last updated July 9, 2020b.

[14] IMF, 2021b, p. 6.

[15] Ludovic Subran, Alexis Garatti, Françoise Huang, and Georges Dib, "The Irony of Biden's Super Stimulus: USD360Bn for Exporters Around the World," Allianz Research, March 15, 2021.

[16] The bill was agreed to after considerable negotiations regarding the size; amounts of up to $2 trillion were proposed (Tony Romm and Seung Min Kim, "Senate Republicans Make New Infrastructure Offer as House Democrats Urge Biden to Dig In," *Washington Post*, May 27, 2021).

[17] White House, Office of Management and Budget, *Budget of the U.S. Government, Fiscal Year 2022*, Washington, D.C., May 28, 2021.

$5.8 trillion in fiscal year 2021. Therefore, making $6 trillion the normal amount spent would be a sizable increase in federal outlays.[18]

Concerns About Debt

Previous stimulus spending and plans under discussion have raised concerns on several dimensions. One is the perennial debate about U.S. federal debt and how much debt the government can accumulate without harming the U.S. economy or the government's own ability to respond to future crises.[19] In early March 2021, before the passage of the American Rescue Plan, the Congressional Budget Office projected that U.S. federal debt held by the public would hit 102 percent of GDP, close to the highest mark since the end of World War II, and an all-time high of 107 percent by 2031 and 202 percent by 2051.[20]

Concerns About Inflation

Beyond that, the stimulus, and the Biden administration's plans to have another large spending bill, raised concerns about inflation, which would particularly harm lower-income people. Several prominent economists, some of them politically aligned with the Biden administration, warned against further spending and said the administration and the Federal Reserve should take steps to make sure the economy does not overheat.[21]

It is not only government spending that is of concern but also the scale of private savings. During the pandemic, people spent less of their income and saved much more. In 2019, total personal savings amounted to $1.2 trillion, or 7.5 percent of personal disposable income. In 2020, those same figures were $2.8 trillion and 16.3 percent. This pace of savings remained in the

---

[18] Spending in fiscal years 2018 through 2020 and projections for spending in fiscal year 2021 are from supplemental data to the U.S. Congressional Budget Office, *The Budget and Economic Outlook: 2021 to 2031*, Washington, D.C., February 11, 2021b.

[19] Howard J. Shatz, "The Long-Term Budget Shortfall and National Security: A Problem the United States Should Stop Avoiding," *War on the Rocks*, November 6, 2017.

[20] U.S. Congressional Budget Office, *The 2021 Long-Term Budget Outlook*, Washington, D.C., March 4, 2021c.

[21] Lawrence H. Summers, "The Inflation Risk Is Real," *Washington Post*, May 24, 2021; Gillian Tett, "When Economic Tribes Go to War," *Financial Times*, May 20, 2021.

first quarter of 2021, when total personal savings amounted to 21 percent of personal disposable income and was on pace to hit $4.1 trillion.[22] The concern was that as the economy opened, people would spend down their savings, further stimulating economic activity. In the second quarter of 2021, personal savings was lower, at an annualized amount of almost $1.9 trillion, but still 10.3 percent of personal disposable income.[23] This was higher than any savings rate after the fourth quarter of 1984 until the second quarter of 2020, when it shot up to 26.1 percent.[24]

The administration has countered that inflation is largely under control and that price rises stem in part from catching up to trend, since prices fell and then rose very slowly during the worst of the pandemic; from temporary supply chain disruptions; and from temporary surges in pent-up demand.[25] Furthermore, as of August 2021, total nonfarm employment was 147.2 million, still 5.3 million below the peak of February 2020.[26] However, there are several reasons why that level might in fact be tight, such as an unusually high number of unfilled job openings and rising wages.[27] This would also argue against further large-scale stimulus and concern about inflation.

One consequence of inflation would be tightening by the Federal Reserve, an action that would increase interest rates. This would then raise the cost of servicing federal debt, and those interest payments would need to come

---

[22] U.S. Bureau of Economic Analysis, "Personal Income and Outlays, March 2021," BEA 21–19, April 30, 2021d.

[23] U.S. Bureau of Economic Analysis, "Personal Income and Outlays, July 2021," BEA 21–41, August 27, 2021g.

[24] U.S. Bureau of Economic Analysis, "Table 2.1. Personal Income and Its Disposition," *National Income and Product Accounts*, interactive data, last updated August 27, 2021h.

[25] Jared Bernstein and Ernie Tedeschi, "Pandemic Prices: Assessing Inflation in the Months and Years Ahead," *Council of Economic Advisers*, blog, White House, April 12, 2021.

[26] This was an improvement from the 144.1 million number in March 2021, or almost 8.5 million below the peak, one year after pandemic shutdowns began (U.S. Bureau of Labor Statistics, 2021).

[27] Robert S. Kaplan, Tyler Atkinson, Jim Dolmas, Marc P. Giannoni, and Karel Mertens, "The Labor Market May Be Tighter than the Level of Employment Suggests," Federal Reserve Bank of Dallas, May 27, 2021.

out of the federal budget, leading to either cuts in other programs or even greater borrowing to maintain programs at current levels.

Concerns About the Dollar

An additional concern is that mounting national debt, the issuance of large amounts of new money, and concomitant increases in inflation could weaken the exchange rate of the dollar, ultimately shaking confidence in the dollar as a global reserve currency.[28]

Although the Federal Reserve has been buying U.S. government debt (holdings of U.S. Treasury securities had risen to more than $5.3 trillion by the end of August 2021), foreigners have not. Net purchases of U.S. Treasury securities flattened starting in August 2019, when they hit $7 trillion. They have remained between $6.8 trillion and $7.2 trillion since then, hitting $7.2 trillion in June 2021.[29]

Concerns About Inequality

One other consequence of the pandemic and U.S. policy has been a continued but more rapid rise in inequality, particularly wealth inequality. Although not directly related to the geoeconomic balance, this might negatively affect U.S. political cohesion and support for foreign policies that might strengthen the country as a whole but disadvantage portions of the population.

Between the last quarter of 2019 and the first quarter of 2021, the net worth of U.S. households and nonprofit organizations rose by $19 trillion, from $117.9 trillion to $136.9 trillion, the largest 15-month increase since 2004.[30] Most of this accrued to households that were already in the upper

---

[28] John Plender, "The Demise of the Dollar? Reserve Currencies in the Era of 'Going Big,'" *Financial Times*, May 25, 2021.

[29] U.S. Department of the Treasury, "Securities (B): Portfolio Holdings of U.S. and Foreign Securities," Treasury International Capital System, undated b. Specific series were "A. Major Foreign Holders of U.S. Treasury Securities (MFH Table) (Monthly)" and "A.2.a. Historical Data: MFH-history tables."

[30] Board of Governors of the Federal Reserve System, *Z.1. Financial Accounts of the United States: Flow of Funds, Balance Sheets, and Integrated Macroeconomic Accounts, First Quarter 2021, Federal Reserve Statistical Release*, Washington, D.C., June 20, 2021d; Nancy Vanden Houten and Gregory Daco, "Research Briefing: Household Wealth Expands, but So Does Inequality," Oxford Economics, July 27, 2021.

tiers of the wealth distribution. According to a slightly different measure, the net wealth of households in the top 1 percent of the wealth distribution increased by $7.1 trillion during that period; for the next 9 percent, that increase was $6.0 trillion; then for the next 40 percent, it was $4.7 trillion; and finally, for the bottom 50 percent, it was $0.6 trillion.[31]

Much of the reason for this was a rise in asset prices, spurred in large part by U.S. Federal Reserve actions keeping interest rates low. An estimated 90 percent in increases in the value of household assets stemmed from price increases rather than the acquisition of new assets. Households in the upper tiers of the distribution were also more likely to save above their trend savings rates.[32] At the same time, because of lockdowns related to COVID-19, workers whose jobs could not be done from home and small businesses that employed them and depended on in-person traffic did poorly.[33] Thus, although the United States in aggregate emerged powerfully from the pandemic, existing inequalities widened.

Vaccination

To the surprise of many, during 2020, an innovative industrial policy program called Operation Warp Speed rapidly accelerated the creation and distribution of vaccines for COVID-19. A partnership between the U.S. Department of Health and Human Services, the U.S. Department of Defense, and the private sector, the program aimed to have vaccines available by January 2021.[34] It

---

[31] Board of Governors of the Federal Reserve System, "Distribution of Household Wealth in the U.S. Since 1989," DFA: Distributional Financial Accounts, online database, last updated June 21, 2021e. Note that the specific households in each of these distributional groups in the first quarter of 2021 might have been different from the specific households in each group in the fourth quarter of 2019, because household wealth might rise and fall differently from that of the overall trend.

[32] Vanden Houten and Daco, 2021, p. 2.

[33] Krishna Kumar, "Split-Screen Recovery from Pandemic Isn't Sustainable," UPI, July 20, 2021c.

[34] U.S. Government Accountability Office, *Operation Warp Speed: Accelerated COVID-19 Vaccine Development Status and Efforts to Address Manufacturing Challenges*, Washington, D.C., GAO-21-319, February 2021; Moncef Slaoui and Matthew

met this goal ahead of schedule, in part by agreeing to more than $12 billion in vaccine-related contracts and spending more than $18 billion overall.[35] The U.S. Food and Drug Administration issued its first emergency use authorization for a COVID-19 vaccine on December 11, 2020 (for the Pfizer-BioNTech vaccine), and then it issued its second on December 18, 2020 (for the Moderna vaccine).[36] Vaccines started to be administered that month.

As a consequence, the United States, having in 2020 become one of the world leaders in recorded per capita COVID-19 deaths, became one of the world leaders in quickly vaccinating its own population. As of January 20, 2021, 4.27 percent of the adult population of the United States had received at least one dose of a COVID-19 vaccine.[37] This rose to 14.88 percent by the end of February 2021 and 29.18 percent by the end of March 2021. On May 30, 2021, the United States hit the halfway point, with 50.15 percent of the population having received one dose. As with stimulus money, this rate of vaccination also provided a boost to economic recovery and performance.

However, for a variety of reasons—including political polarization, vaccine hesitancy given reported side effects or other reasons, and poor messaging by U.S. authorities—the rate of vaccinations decelerated during the summer of 2021. On July 15, 2021, the percentage of people in the EU receiving at least one dose surpassed that in the United States for the first time in the pandemic. As of August 31, 2021, 60.96 percent of the U.S. population had received one dose, only an 11 percentage point increase since the end of May 2021.[38] Public health measures, such as requiring masking indoors,

---

Hepburn, "Developing Safe and Effective Covid Vaccines—Operation Warp Speed's Strategy and Approach," *New England Journal of Medicine*, Vol. 383, No. 18, October 29, 2020; David Shulkin, "What Health Care Can Learn from Operation Warp Speed," commentary, *NEJM Catalyst*, January 21, 2021.

[35] Stephanie Baker and Cynthia Koons, "Inside Operation Warp Speed's $18 Billion Sprint for a Vaccine," *Bloomberg*, October 29, 2020.

[36] U.S. Food and Drug Administration, "Emergency Use Authorization," webpage, last updated June 7, 2021. A third authorization was issued on February 27, 2021, for the Janssen (Johnson and Johnson) vaccine.

[37] Our World in Data, undated; data accessed June 7, 2021.

[38] Our World in Data, undated; data accessed September 1, 2021.

were renewed in various states, as were public health messaging and outreach encouraging people to get vaccinated.

Conclusion

By summer 2021, the United States in aggregate had emerged strongly from both the disease and the economic consequences of the response to the disease. The vaccination rate was high but flattening and included some differences among various populations. Furthermore, national GDP surpassed 2019's high mark. With an administration publicly committed to working with allies and partners, this put the United States in a strong position to lead the global recovery.

But risks remained. Most notably, the economic response to the disease and then spending plans under the new administration held the potential to strongly boost growth but also inflation and dramatically increase federal debt, a long-standing problem that successive administrations had failed to control. Furthermore, the spread of the delta variant was causing an increase in illnesses, especially among the unvaccinated, and inequality had widened with the potential to increase further if lockdowns were reinstated and if policies supportive to asset price growth were to continue. These disparities could affect the robustness and the stability of the recovery, policymaking, and future resource allocation, especially in a highly polarized political environment.

CHAPTER FOUR

COVID-19 and U.S. Competitors

Both China and Russia fared better economically than initially expected. In addition, both at least initially gained geopolitical advantage through vaccine diplomacy. However, both are facing difficult aftereffects, and it is still too early to say whether vaccine diplomacy efforts will yield longer-term advantage.

China

China was the only major economy to grow in 2020, and its annual GDP was up 2.3 percent from GDP in 2019. Growth accelerated during the year, and by the fourth quarter of 2020, GDP was 6.5 percent above fourth quarter 2019 GDP and 3.2 percent above third quarter 2020 GDP. According to one projection, GDP was expected to increase by a further 8.1 percent in 2021.[1] China also embarked on a major vaccine development effort that led to 20 vaccines in clinical trials and two approved by the World Health Organization for worldwide use by June 2021. In China itself, the National Health Commission reported that more than 704.8 million doses had been administered as of June 3, 2021, and by August 31, 2021, this had risen to 2.05 billion doses—more than one per person.[2] The releases do not indicate

---

[1] IMF, 2021b, p. 6.

[2] National Health Commission of the People's Republic of China, "Over 700 Mln COVID-19 Vaccine Doses Administered Across China," Xinhua, June 4, 2021a; National Health Commission of the People's Republic of China, "Over 2.05 Bln Doses of COVID-19 Vaccines Administered in China," Xinhua, September 1, 2021b.

what percentage of China's population of 1.4 billion people had received at least one dose.

Although China and the United States both experienced GDP changes in 2020 that were more positive than those of their peer group, China did much better. The gap between China's full-year 2019 GDP growth and U.S. full-year 2019 GDP growth was 3.8 percentage points (6.0 percent for China versus 2.2 percent for the United States). In contrast, the gap for full-year 2020 growth was 5.8 percentage points (2.3 percent for China versus –3.5 percent for the United States).[3] Furthermore, even with the pandemic, China announced that it had met its goal of eliminating absolute poverty by the end of 2020 one month early, in November 2020.[4]

The origin of the pandemic in China and China's lack of transparency about it inspired a certain degree of anger worldwide in 2020, along with discussion of selective decoupling in specific sectors.[5] This lack of transparency continued into 2021 as evidence became more public that experiments in a Chinese laboratory funded in part by the United States were one possible origin of the novel coronavirus.[6] In the summer of 2021, China rejected any new investigations that did not use a heavily disputed February 2020 report as their basis.[7] Although the envisioned economic decoupling might be in process, at least to a limited extent, China's international goods trade

---

[3] National Bureau of Statistics of China, "Announcement of the National Bureau of Statistics on the Final Verification of GDP in 2019," press release, Beijing, December 30, 2020; National Bureau of Statistics of China, "Statistical Communiqué of the People's Republic of China on the 2020 National Economic and Social Development," press release, Beijing, February 28, 2021b; U.S. Bureau of Economic Analysis, "Gross Domestic Product, First Quarter 2021 (Advance Estimate)," news release, Suitland, Md., BEA 21–18, April 29, 2021c.

[4] "China Removes All Remaining Counties from Poverty List," Xinhua, November 23, 2020.

[5] Howard J. Shatz, "COVID-19 and Economic Competition with China and Russia," *War on the Rocks*, August 31, 2020.

[6] Nicholas Wade, "The Origin of COVID: Did People or Nature Open Pandora's Box at Wuhan?" *Bulletin of the Atomic Scientists*, May 5, 2021.

[7] "China Rejects WHO Call for Renewed Probe into Origins of COVID-19," *France 24*, August 13, 2021; Gabriel Crossley, "China Rejects WHO Plan for Study of COVID-19 Origin," Reuters, July 22, 2021.

rose in 2020 to its highest point ever in nominal terms in both renminbi (RMB) and dollars. Combined exports plus imports hit almost $4.66 trillion, 1.9 percent higher than in 2019.[8]

Trouble Behind the Growth Numbers

Even as China grew, this growth set the country back in its efforts to reform its economy. In addition, several other problems remained. Notably, although growth continued in the first quarter of 2021, it signaled a slowing of the Chinese economy relative to performance before the pandemic. GDP jumped by an eye-popping 18.3 percent relative to the first quarter of 2020, but analysts had expected growth of 19.2 percent.[9]

Furthermore, first quarter 2021 growth rose only 0.6 percent relative to fourth quarter 2020, the lowest rate of quarterly growth since at least the first quarter of 2011 (excluding the dramatic decline in the first quarter of 2020 that was caused by COVID-19).[10] The average annual rate from the first quarter of 2019 to the first quarter of 2021 was only 5.0 percent, well below the rates in the 6 percent to 7 percent range that China had been registering. This slow growth continued into the second quarter, with GDP in that quarter growing 1.3 percent relative to the first quarter of 2021.[11] That is the lowest second quarter growth China has had since at least 2016, and it is lower than all but three quarterly growth rates since the beginning of 2016.

Beyond the slower growth, the type of growth that China experienced in 2020 was a setback to its reform plans. China has been working to reform its

---

[8] National Bureau of Statistics of China, 2021b. The RMB value was 32.16 trillion. RMB values were converted at an average annual 2020 exchange rate of 6.9042 RMB to the U.S. dollar (Board of Governors of the Federal Reserve System, "China / U.S. Foreign Exchange Rate [DEXCHUS]," FRED, Federal Reserve Bank of St. Louis, last updated May 24, 2021a).

[9] Jonathan Cheng, "Chinese Economy Grew More than 18% in First Quarter," *Wall Street Journal*, April 16, 2021b.

[10] National Bureau of Statistics of China, 2021c; National Bureau of Statistics of China, "Gross Domestic Product? Growth Rate (Preceding Quarter = 100)(%)," webpage, undated.

[11] National Bureau of Statistics of China, "Preliminary Accounting Results of GDP for the Second Quarter and the First Half Year of 2021," webpage, July 19, 2021d.

economy in two related ways. First, it has been trying to move from an export- and investment-led economy to a more consumption- and innovation-led economy. Second, and related, it has been trying to lower its debt relative to GDP, because a large share of its growth in the decade of the 2010s—based on the export- and investment-led model—has come from debt-fueled, inefficient investment. For example, in 2017, President Xi Jinping noted that the Chinese economy "has been transitioning from a phase of rapid growth to a stage of high-quality development," and he identified the need to develop "drivers of growth in medium-high end consumption, innovation-driven development," and several other elements of the economy.[12]

China had been succeeding modestly at both of these goals. However, the 2020 growth was marked by retrogression. Final consumption expenditure contributed –0.5 percentage points to 2020 growth, whereas gross capital formation (a measure of investment) contributed 2.2 percentage points and net exports contributed 0.7 percentage points, meaning exports rose relative to imports.[13] In addition, debt relative to GDP rose by 20 percentage points to its highest level ever, 272 percent of GDP.[14] China has seemed to stabilize debt, if not reverse it, holding it to 247 percent of GDP in 2019, up only 2 percentage points from 2018's 245 percent. In the first quarter of 2021, China managed to bring debt down to 269 percent of GDP, but that was still more than 20 percentage points above the 2019 mark and more than 30 percentage points above the 2017 mark.[15]

Signs of problems show up beyond the growth data. Although the size of China's economy is now larger than it was before COVID-19, the number of migrant workers who traveled to cities for employment in the first quar-

---

[12] Xi Jinping, "Secure a Decisive Victory in Building a Moderately Prosperous Society in All Respects and Strive for the Great Success of Socialism with Chinese Characteristics for a New Era," speech delivered at the 19th National Congress of the Communist Party of China, Beijing, October 18, 2017.

[13] National Bureau of Statistics of China, 2021b.

[14] Alicia Garcia-Herrero, "China's Debt Surge Moderated in Q4 2020 but Scars in Terms of Long-Term Growth Impact to Remain," LinkedIn Pulse, February 5, 2021a. Garcia-Herrero is the chief economist for Asia Pacific at Natixis.

[15] Alicia Garcia-Herrero, "China's Strong Growth in Q1 Helped Debt Dynamics but for How Long?" LinkedIn Pulse, April 30, 2021b.

ter of 2021 was 2.5 million lower than before the pandemic hit, and youth unemployment was slightly higher.[16] Small businesses were also reported to be struggling. The source of 80 percent of urban jobs, small businesses still faced higher-than-normal cash flow constraints as of early May 2021.[17]

Even the landmark poverty reduction achievement is not all that it seems. An upper-middle income country, China chose a poverty line of $2.25 per day, somewhere between that appropriate for a lower-income country, such as Ethiopia ($1.90 per day), and a lower-middle income country, such as India ($3.20 per day), rather than the more appropriate $5.50 per day.[18] Under this threshold, although China might have eliminated abject poverty, tens of millions if not hundreds of millions of people remain extremely poor. Furthermore, the cost of the effort has been put at $800 billion or more, raising questions about its sustainability should China's economy run into trouble or future Chinese leaders find they have other priorities. Methods through which the poverty reduction has come about have also been an issue. Forced relocations from isolated villages to larger towns have led to some discontent among those for whom poverty has been alleviated.[19]

Closed Borders for COVID-19

Although China seemed successful at countering the COVID-19 pandemic in 2020, it still faces challenges. In large part, these stem from a declared zero-tolerance for COVID-19—that is, a decision to completely eliminate COVID-19. This has led to strong external and internal barriers. China has maintained strong limits on foreigners entering the country, and the deputy head of the National Health Commission, Li Bin, was quoted as

---

[16] Jonathan Cheng, "China Growth Numbers Betray Waning Momentum," *Wall Street Journal*, April 16, 2021a.

[17] Stella Yifan Xie, "For China's Small Businesses, Life Is Still Far from Normal," *Wall Street Journal*, May 2, 2021a.

[18] Indermit Gill, "Deep-Sixing Poverty in China," *Future Development*, blog, Brookings Institution, January 25, 2021. Prices are real 2011 values adjusted for purchasing power parity, an adjustment that takes account of the fact that different goods and services have different prices across countries.

[19] Alice Su, "China Fulfills a Dream to End Poverty. Not All Poor People Are Feeling Better Off," *Los Angeles Times*, November 27, 2020.

saying, "All outbreaks are sparked by imported cases, so our main job for now is to prevent reintroductions."[20]

Throughout the spring and summer of 2021, China dealt with periodic outbreaks that led to localized or regional restrictions on activity. For example, with an outbreak in the city of Nanjing, officials set up 68 roadblocks at city boundaries, requiring exiting drivers to present a negative nucleic acid test result and a green health code to exit.[21] China has been using color-coded health apps since February 2020.[22] In early August 2021, when the delta variant was spreading through China as in many other countries, China had suspended flights from Nanjing and nearby Yangzhou and canceled trains from 23 cities to Beijing. People were barred from leaving Zhangjiajie, a city of 1.5 million people southwest of Shanghai, and discouraged from leaving Beijing and the southern province of Guangdong.[23]

These restrictions have raised concerns that China's continued economic recovery from COVID-19 will be slower than expected. Restrictions have slowed down port operations, and the consequences have affected not only China's economy but also the global economy because of China's centrality in global supply chains.[24] In early August 2021, both Goldman Sachs and Morgan Stanley cut their GDP growth estimates for 2021.[25] That same month, China's nonmanufacturing purchasing managers' index (PMI) fell to 47.5 from 53.3 in July 2021, with any number below 50 indicating a contraction. The services PMI, part of the nonmanufacturing PMI, fell to 45.2 in August 2021 from 52.5 in July 2021. Officials noted the cause of

---

[20] As quoted in Christian Shepherd and Primrose Riordan, "China Lacks Covid Exit Strategy as It Strives for Zero Infections," *Financial Times*, July 20, 2021.

[21] European Union Chamber of Commerce in China, "COVID-19 Travel Control in Nanjing," Voice of European Business in China, email update, July 29, 2021.

[22] Laney Zhang, "China: Health QR Code Now Required for Foreigners Flying to China," *Global Legal Monitor*, Library of Congress, December 14, 2020.

[23] Joe McDonald and Huizhong Wu, "Delta Variant Challenges China's Costly Lockdown Strategy," Associated Press, August 5, 2021.

[24] "Chinese Ports Choke over China's 'Zero Tolerance' COVID-19 Policy," Reuters, August 17, 2021.

[25] Stella Yifan Xie, "China's Strict Covid-19 Strategy Risks Slowing Economic Recovery as Delta Variant Hits," *Wall Street Journal*, August 10, 2021b.

the decline in the nonmanufacturing index as "recent multi provincial and multi-point epidemic and other factors."[26]

Russia

Like China, Russia performed far better economically than initially expected. The Bank of Russia estimated that the Russian economy had reached its prepandemic level in the second quarter of 2021, with demand for labor growing throughout the economy.[27]

In its most negative projection, in June 2020 the IMF projected Russia's full-year growth at –6.6 percent, but the country's GDP ended up falling by only 3.0 percent. Russian statistical authorities estimated that 2021 first quarter GDP was 99.3 percent that of first quarter 2020, indicating that the pace of decline had slowed.[28] This was the fourth quarter of decline, but the decrease of less than 1 percent was better than the decrease of 1.8 percent in the fourth quarter of 2020 relative to the same quarter in 2019.[29] The preliminary figure for 2021 second quarter GDP was estimated to be 110.3 percent above 2020 second quarter GDP; the 2020 quarter was the quarter of the largest decline and was therefore a low base when calculating growth.[30]

---

[26] National Bureau of Statistics of China, "Purchasing Managers Index for August 2021," webpage, September 1, 2021e.

[27] Bank of Russia, "The Bank of Russia Increases the Key Rate by 100 b.p., to 6.50% p.a.," press release, Moscow, July 23, 2021b.

[28] Federal State Statistical Service (Rosstat), "On the Production of Gross Domestic Product (GDP) in the First Quarter of 2021" ["О производстве валового внутреннего продукта (ВВП) в I квартале 2021 года"], News of Rosstat, June 15, 2021e. The preliminary estimate of 2021 first quarter GDP released in May 2021 recorded GDP as 99 percent of that of first quarter 2020, indicating that Russia had performed better than initially expected (Federal State Statistical Service (Rosstat), "Rosstat Presents a Preliminary Estimate of GDP for the 1st Quarter of 2021" ["Росстат представляет предварительную оценку ВВП за I квартал 2021 года"], News of Rosstat, May 17, 2021d).

[29] Focus Economics, "Russia: Pace of Economic Contraction Softens in Q1," May 17, 2021.

[30] Federal State Statistical Service (Rosstat), "On a Preliminary Estimate of the Dynamics of GDP in the Second Quarter of 2021" ["О предварительной оценке динамики ВВП во II квартале 2021 года"], News of Rosstat, August 13, 2021f.

Initially slow to provide policy support for the economic downturn, Russia eventually supplied fiscal support of between 3.5 percent and 4.5 percent of GDP. In addition, the Bank of Russia cut the policy interest rate to 4.25 percent, a historic low, and gave banks greater leeway to support businesses.[31]

Russia also increased its macroeconomic buffers during the pandemic. Russia's international reserves totaled $554 billion at the end of December 2019 and, despite some modest fluctuations, totaled $596 billion at the end of December 2020. More recently, they were $601 billion at the end of July 2021.[32] Likewise, Russia's National Wealth Fund increased 13.7 percent in dollar terms from April 2020 to August 2021 to $188.1 billion and 7.0 percent in ruble terms, indicating ruble appreciation. The August 2021 total amounted to 11.9 percent of GDP.[33] As of April 2021, the IMF expected Russia's economy to grow 3.8 percent in both 2021 and 2022, but by July 2021, the IMF had raised the 2021 estimate to 4.4 percent and lowered the 2022 estimate to 3.1 percent.[34]

Russia's Energy Economy and Future Development Plans

One of the reasons that Russia suffered during the pandemic was that oil prices crashed, falling from a monthly average price per barrel of $63.65 in January 2020 to $18.38 in April 2020.[35] The initial decline was brought on in part by a dispute between Saudi Arabia and Russia, in which Saudi

---

[31] IMF, "Russian Federation," Policy Responses to COVID-19: Policy Tracker, webpage, last updated May 7, 2021c.

[32] Bank of Russia, "International Reserves of the Russian Federation (End of Period)," database, last updated August 1, 2021a.

[33] Ministry of Finance of the Russian Federation, "Volume of the National Wealth Fund," Statistics, webpage, last updated August 9, 2021b. April 2020 is used as the base year because the fund saw a large jump from March 2020 to April 2020 (34.3 percent in dollar terms and 55.8 percent in ruble terms) but then steadier changes afterward.

[34] IMF, *World Economic Outlook Update: Fault Lines Widen in the Global Recovery,* Washington, D.C., July 2021d.

[35] U.S. Energy Information Administration, "Europe Brent Spot Price FOB (Dollars Per Barrel)," data sourced from Thomson Reuters, release date May 19, 2021.

Arabia wanted coordinated production cuts to maintain prices but Russia disagreed—in part to see whether the effects of COVID-19 would be temporary and in part as a component of a longer-term effort to hurt higher-cost U.S. shale oil production, which had kept global oil prices low for years.[36] Lower prices would have brought about short-term pain for Russia in return for longer-term geopolitical goals. The tactic boomeranged, however, as Saudi Arabia turned on the taps and drove prices even lower. The Kremlin then retreated and agreed to a new deal with Saudi Arabia in April 2020, brokered by President Trump.[37] Prices rebounded into the low $40s from June 2020 through November 2020, still lower than they had been before COVID-19. Demand for energy was low because of reduced economic activity. Worldwide, oil demand fell 8.8 percent, the largest amount ever recorded.[38] Natural gas demand fell by 1.9 percent.[39]

This had implications for the Russian budget. Between 2006 and 2019, oil and gas revenues constituted an annual average of 44.5 percent of federal budget revenues.[40] This percentage rose during periods of high oil prices, such as 2011 through 2014, when the annual share averaged 50.3 percent (oil prices started a large decline in late 2014). And it fell during periods of low oil prices, such as 2015 through 2017, when the annual share averaged 39.5 percent.

In 2020, according to preliminary data, oil and gas revenues to the federal budget were at their lowest since 2016 and their second lowest since 2010. Accordingly, their contribution to federal budget revenues totaled only 28.0 percent. Combined with additional spending to respond to the

---

[36] Benoit Faucon, Georgi Kantchev, and Summer Said, "Russia Takes Aim at U.S. Shale Oil Producers," *Wall Street Journal*, March 13, 2020.

[37] Clifford Krauss, "Oil Nations, Prodded by Trump, Reach Deal to Slash Production," *New York Times*, April 12, 2020.

[38] International Energy Agency, *Global Energy Review 2021*, Paris, April 2021, p. 14.

[39] International Energy Agency, 2021, p. 20.

[40] Ministry of Finance of the Russian Federation, "Annual Report on Execution of the Federal Budget (Starting from January 1, 2006)," Federal Budget of the Russian Federation, webpage, last updated April 15, 2021a. Note that oil and gas revenues are a much smaller share of the consolidated budget, combining the budgets of the federal government and the regions.

economic consequences of COVID-19, the budget hit its largest deficit since at least 2006. As of mid-May 2021, oil prices were at levels similar to 2019 prices, so the Russian federal budget might move closer to balance. However, spending was likely to go down in 2021; it jumped from 18.2 trillion rubles in 2019 to a record high of 22.8 trillion rubles in 2020, whereas it had been in the 16 trillion to 17 trillion ruble range from 2016 through 2018.

One of the main consequences of the pandemic was the reshaping of Russia's flagship development effort, the 12 National Projects. Announced in 2018, they were to last through 2024 and amount to $360 billion to $400 billion, depending on the exchange rate, and almost half was to be spent on infrastructure.[41] Even in 2019, however, the ambition outstripped the ability to execute, and in January 2020 Mikhail Mishustin replaced Dmitry Medvedev as prime minister in a move seen by some as an effort to get the National Projects moving again. Later that year, the government opted to stretch out implementation through 2030.[42] And in early 2021, Russia was again reportedly redesigning its National Projects.[43]

Other development plans are afoot. In his annual address to the Federal Assembly, President Vladimir Putin noted how the pandemic had exacerbated problems of social inequality and poverty (worldwide, although his focus was Russia).[44] He also noted Russia's demographic challenges; these include an aging and declining population.[45] Accordingly, he outlined a set of

---

[41] "Putin's 'Great Society' Program: Russian Government Outlines 12 Major National Projects," TASS, February 11, 2019; Natalia Orlova, "Russian National Projects During the Crisis Period," *Expert Opinions*, Valdai Discussion Club blog, May 1, 2020; Jake Cordell, "State-Run Bank Says Russia Unlikely to Meet Economic Targets 'Without More Active Policies,'" *Moscow Times*, November 20, 2019. In national currency terms, the total budget was estimated at 26 trillion rubles (Orlova, 2020).

[42] "Russia Resets Ambitious National Development Plan," *Moscow Times*, July 13, 2020.

[43] Ben Aris, "Russian Government Launches a National Projects 2.0 Revamp," BNE Intellinews, February 5, 2021.

[44] Vladimir Putin, "Message from the President to the Federal Assembly," Moscow, April 21, 2021.

[45] Russia's population is projected to decline from 146 million in 2020 to 136 million by 2050 (United Nations, Department of Economic and Social Affairs, Population Division, "World Population Prospects 2019," online database, 2019). Many countries in Europe and elsewhere face similar demographic challenges.

policies that would better support families and children, specifying that each of the 12 National Projects should include policies to support young people. Economic policy directions included simplification of rules and regulations; support for private investment and entrepreneurs; tax reforms; infrastructure investment, especially in light of the government's significant financial reserves in the National Wealth Fund; and support for regions, especially in infrastructure and transportation connectivity. Notably, as did leaders in many other governments, Putin highlighted the importance of limited decoupling from the rest of the world and bringing supply chains back to Russia, particularly in the production of vaccines and other pharmaceuticals.

As of the writing of this report, Russia's near-term budget outlook was positive. Not only was the National Wealth Fund higher than before the pandemic but also global oil demand was projected to rise by 6.2 percent in 2021 (although it would remain 3 percent below 2019 levels).[46] Furthermore, natural gas demand was projected to rise by 3.2 percent in 2021, resulting in total demand 1.3 percent above that of 2019.[47]

Challenges to Recovery and Growth

Despite the positive outlook, there are various headwinds. As in much of the world, economic performance in Russia was uneven, with job losses concentrated in manufacturing, construction, retail and hospitality, and health and social services, the first three of which were sectors most susceptible to lockdown effects.[48] These sectors' large job losses also had the largest real wage losses. Even though the economy had recovered by June 2020 to its level at the end of 2019, oil production had not recovered to pre-COVID-19 levels because of production agreements among the Organization of Petroleum

---

[46] International Energy Agency, 2021, p. 2. Elsewhere, the report said that global oil demand was set to rise 6.0 percent but stay 3.2 percent below 2019 levels (p. 14).

[47] International Energy Agency, 2021, p. 20.

[48] World Bank Group, *Russia's Economic Recovery Gathers Pace: Special Focus on Cost-Effective Safety Nets*, Washington, D.C., No. 45, May 2021, p. 30.

Exporting Countries, Russia, and other oil producers; air travel remained at lower levels, and services had not rebounded.[49]

In addition, Russia's vaccination rates have been very low. Even though Russia developed its own vaccine that is being distributed globally, the Sputnik V, and in fact was the first country to announce a vaccine, only 11.36 percent of its population had received one vaccine dose as of May 31, 2021.[50] This was barely above the global average of 10.77 percent on the same date. Reported causes include low expectations of becoming ill with COVID-19, lack of trust in authorities, preference for foreign medicine, and skepticism about the Russian vaccine's rapid development.[51]

In response, de facto mandatory vaccine requirements started appearing. In the summer of 2021, the city of Moscow required vaccines for a wide variety of people, with regions adopting similar policies. Moscow also instituted a QR-code system, with customers of cafés and restaurants required to show proof of vaccine, other proof of immunity, or a negative test.[52] Likewise, threats of penalties were floated for retail and service businesses with fewer than 60 percent of their employees vaccinated.[53] By August 31, 2021, 30.00 percent of the Russian population had received at least one dose, almost a 20 percentage point increase from the figure only three months earlier.[54]

Over the longer term, various redevelopment policies might well contribute to Russian growth, although there is some question about whether they will be implemented. Russia has gone through 20 years of announcements of major plans, including the Program for the Socio-Economic

---

[49] Darya Korsunskaya, "Update 1—Russia's Economy Ministry Proposes Extra State Spending to Offset Rate Hikes," Reuters, August 5, 2021.

[50] Our World in Data, undated; data accessed September 1, 2021.

[51] Felix Light, "Will Russia's Belated Promotion of Sputnik V at Home Sway a Doubting Public?" *Moscow Times*, April 7, 2021; Georgi Kantchev, "Russia's COVID-19 Vaccine Is Embraced Abroad, Snubbed at Home," *Wall Street Journal*, March 8, 2021.

[52] Andrey Ostroukh, "Russia's Economic Recovery Faces COVID-19, Inflation Headwinds," Reuters, July 5, 2021.

[53] Robyn Dixon, "Vaccine-Skippers Face Work Penalties," *Washington Post*, July 29, 2021, p. A15.

[54] Our World in Data, undated; data accessed September 1, 2021.

Development of the Russian Federation for the Period 2000–2010, known as the Gref Plan, introduced in 2000; the Concept for the Long-Term Socio-Economic Development of the Russian Federation until 2020, introduced in 2008; Strategy 2020, introduced in May 2012; and the National Projects, introduced in May 2018.[55] However, there is little to show for these planned projects, and the need for reform and investment is still high, as Putin noted in his April 2021 address.

Conclusion

As it did worldwide, the COVID-19 pandemic damaged the economies of China and Russia. China experienced its lowest growth in decades, and Russia ended up delaying its flagship development program by six years, although COVID-19 was not the sole or even most important cause of Russia's delay.

At least by summer 2021, COVID-19 had not altered China's or Russia's relative rankings in the global economy. Before the pandemic, China was the fastest-growing major economy but faced serious domestic imbalances; Russia was a slow-growth, demographically challenged economy highly dependent on the production and sale of hydrocarbons. For both countries, all of this remained true after the pandemic.

---

[55] Ben Aris and Ivan Tkachev, "Long Read: 20 Years of Russia's Economy Under Putin, in Numbers," *Moscow Times*, August 19, 2019.

CHAPTER FIVE

COVID-19 and U.S. Allies and Partners

The countries of the EU as a group, the UK, and Japan all experienced larger declines in economic activity than did the United States, although there was significant variation among them. This extended a long-standing trend in which the share of global GDP produced by U.S. allies and partners has been declining, while that of the United States has been holding steady or declining more slowly and that of China has been rising.[1] India suffered a significant decline, temporarily reversing its growth path, while Australia performed relatively better than most advanced countries but instituted strict lockdowns and border controls to manage the spread of the disease.

The European Union

The EU, and especially northern Italy, was the first site of the large-scale appearance of COVID-19 outside China. By early March 2020, Italy had placed 16 million people under quarantine.[2] Countries handled the pandemic differently, but the pandemic proved to be economically devastating to the European bloc as a whole in 2020. GDP in the 27 countries of the EU declined by 6.2 percent in 2020 and by 6.6 percent among the 19 countries of the euro area. This was actually better than expected. In its April 2020 outlook, the IMF projected that the economy of the euro area would decline

---

[1] Shatz and Chandler, 2020.

[2] "Coronavirus: Northern Italy Quarantines 16 Million People," BBC, March 8, 2020.

by 7.5 percent. The IMF then became more pessimistic with its June 2020 outlook, projecting a 10.2 percent decline.

Economic performance within the EU was highly variable, with the southern countries generally doing worse. This stemmed in part from their reliance on tourism and the cancellation of the tourist economy in 2020. For example, 2020 GDP relative to 2019 GDP was down 11.0 percent in Spain, 8.9 percent in Italy, 8.2 percent in Greece, and 8.1 percent in France. In contrast, it was down 4.9 percent in Germany, 3.8 percent in the Netherlands, 2.8 percent in Denmark, and 2.7 percent in Poland. This pattern was strong but not universal—GDP fell 6.6 percent in Austria and 6.5 percent in Belgium, but except for Cyprus (down 5.1 percent), every southern EU country bordering the Atlantic Ocean, Mediterranean Sea, Adriatic Sea, or Aegean Sea performed worse than the EU average.[3]

As with nearly all countries, the EU's worst quarter was the second quarter of 2020, with growth rebounding in the third quarter. However, from there, the EU's economy went negative again, diverging from the economy of the United States. The EU's economy fell by 0.4 percent in the fourth quarter of 2020 relative to the third quarter, and then fell again by 0.1 percent in the first quarter of 2021, relative to the fourth quarter of 2020. These numbers were more negative for the euro area, down 0.6 percent and 0.3 percent for the fourth quarter of 2020 and the first quarter of 2021, respectively.[4] By the second quarter of 2020, the EU had once again returned to growth, indicated by an early estimate of a 1.9 percent increase in GDP relative to that of the first quarter for the EU and a 2.0 percent increase for the euro area. However, this still left EU-wide GDP 2.6 percent below its seasonally adjusted high that had been reached in the fourth quarter of 2019.

Compounding these problems, the EU was slow to embark on a vaccination program, which might partly explain the negative economic perfor-

---

[3] Eurostat, 2021a; extracted April 2, 2021, Brussels time, April 1, 2021, U.S. time.

[4] Eurostat, "GDP Up by 2.0% and Employment Up by 0.5% in the Euro Area," GDP and Employment Flash Estimates for the Second Quarter of 2021, 94/2021, August 17, 2021e. Initial estimates were actually more negative (Eurostat, "GDP Down by 0.6% and Employment Down by 0.3% in the Euro Area; in the EU, GDP Down by 0.4% and Employment Down by 0.3%," GDP and Employment Flash Estimates for the First Quarter of 2021, 58/2021, May 18, 2021d).

mance at the beginning of 2021. Beyond the slow start, there was a degree of vaccine skepticism in parts of Europe, including France and Germany.[5] As an example of the low rate of vaccinations, on April 15, 2021, 37.62 percent of the U.S. population had received at least one dose of a coronavirus vaccine. For the EU on this same date, the share was 17.5 percent. But by May 2021, the EU's pace had started to increase.[6] On July 14, 2021—the French national holiday Bastille Day—vaccinations in the EU surpassed those in the United States: 55.02 percent of people in the EU had received at least one dose compared with 54.96 percent in the United States.[7] By August 31, 2021, these figures were 64.49 percent for the EU and 60.96 for the United States.[8] This increase in vaccination rates might have stemmed from mandates for some groups of workers and threats of restrictions on unvaccinated people.[9]

EU performance differed in one other notable way from that of the United States. Both economies experienced similar declines in total hours worked. However, in the United States, this came primarily from the loss of jobs. In the EU, it came primarily from declines in hours worked by people who retained their jobs.[10] This stemmed from the extension of existing programs and the start of new programs paying for companies to retain workers who might have no or only part-time work.[11] Employment in the 27 members of the EU peaked at 191.4 million in the fourth quarter of 2019 and had fallen to 186.6 million in the second quarter of 2020, a decline of

---

[5] Rick Noack, "Vaccine-Skeptic France, Germany Inch Toward Near-Mandates," *Washington Post*, July 18, 2021, p. A24.

[6] Marcus Walker and Bojan Pancevski, "Troubled Covid-19 Vaccine Rollout in Europe Nears Possible Turning Point," *Wall Street Journal*, April 9, 2021; Bertrand Benoit, Giovanni Legorano, and Nick Kostov, "Europe's Troubled COVID-19 Vaccine Rollout Turns the Corner," *Wall Street Journal*, May 4, 2021.

[7] Our World in Data, undated; data accessed September 1, 2021.

[8] Our World in Data, undated; data accessed September 1, 2021.

[9] Noack, 2021, p. A24.

[10] IMF, *Regional Economic Outlook Update: Europe*, Washington, D.C., April 2021a, p. 3.

[11] Tom Fairless and Paul Hannon, "Europe's Economic Recipe for the Pandemic: Keep Workers in Their Jobs," *Wall Street Journal*, March 24, 2020.

only 4.8 million (monthly figures appear to not be available). Employment then started rising the next quarter.[12]

The pandemic did introduce one major change in EU economic management that might have much longer-term consequences. As part of its *Next-GenerationEU* recovery plan, the EU agreed to issue €750 billion in EU-wide bonds and then grant or loan the money at low interest rates to member countries.[13] The EU had borrowed collectively before but not in such a large amount—in large part because members had resisted turning the organization into more of a fiscal union, in which richer countries could be held responsible for the debts of poorer countries. This new debt issuance will not only help fund recovery but also create low-risk instruments that might attract investors and sovereign debt holders and heighten the use of the euro as a reserve currency.[14]

The United Kingdom and Non-U.S. Members of the Quad: Japan, Australia, and India

The UK and Australia have long been among the closest allies of the United States. Japan became an important treaty ally following its defeat in World War II. More recently, Australia, India, Japan, and the United States have been acting together as the Quadrilateral Security Dialogue, or Quad, to ensure a free and open Indo-Pacific and most recently, to address issues related to COVID-19.[15] Given the close security and economic relations

---

[12] Eurostat, "Employment and Activity by Sex and Age—Quarterly Data [LFSI_EMP_Q__custom_1010160] (Seasonally Adjusted Data Not Calendar Adjusted Data)," spreadsheet from online database, last updated April 13, 2021c.

[13] European Commission, "Recovery Plan for Europe," webpage, undated; European Commission, "Europe's Moment: Repair and Prepare for the Next Generation," press release, Brussels, May 27, 2020.

[14] Jon Rees and Rehan Ahmad, "EU Will Be Big New Player in Bond Market with Likely Triple-A Asset," S&P Global, August 3, 2020.

[15] White House, "Quad Leaders' Joint Statement: 'The Spirit of the Quad,'" Washington, D.C., March 12, 2021d.

these countries have with the United States, the way COVID-19 has affected them has implications for U.S. security and economic well-being.

UK economic performance in 2020 was by far the worst among the G-7 major advanced economies, even worse than that of Italy, the first epicenter of COVID-19 in Europe. UK GDP fell 19.5 percent in the second quarter of 2020 relative to the first quarter, rebounded 16.9 percent in the third quarter, and had further, smaller positive change in the fourth quarter.[16] The UK ended 2020 with annual GDP 9.8 percent below that of 2019. And although momentum was positive in the second half of 2020, the UK turned downward in early 2021 (like the EU economy), falling 1.6 percent in the first quarter relative to the last quarter of 2020.[17] In contrast to all major economies, the UK economy experienced robust growth in the second quarter of 2021, rising 4.8 percent relative to the first quarter. However, this still left it 4.4 percent below its high mark set in the fourth quarter of 2019.[18]

High rates of disease incidence and lockdowns drove the UK's 2020 economic result, compounding the effects of uncertainty over the UK's future economic relationship with the EU as a consequence of Brexit.[19] Where the UK differed from most other advanced industrial economies was in its vaccination efforts. Besides subsidizing the development of the

---

[16] Office for National Statistics (United Kingdom), 2021a. UK second quarter 2020 GDP was 21.4 percent below second quarter 2019 GDP.

[17] Office for National Statistics (United Kingdom), "GDP First Quarterly Estimate, UK: April to June 2021," statistical bulletin, August 12, 2021c. The initial first quarter estimate was a decrease of 1.5 percent (Office for National Statistics (United Kingdom), "GDP First Quarterly Estimate, UK: January to March 2021," statistical bulletin, May 12, 2021b).

[18] Office for National Statistics (United Kingdom), 2021c.

[19] The UK left the EU on January 31, 2020, but maintained its pre-Brexit trade relations until a new Trade and Cooperation Agreement took effect provisionally on January 1, 2021, and fully on May 1, 2021. The agreement was under negotiation for much of 2020, and uncertainty about the future relationship during the entire period after the Brexit referendum had negative consequences for UK growth (Charles P. Ries, Marco Hafner, Clement Fays, and Erez Yerushalmi, *The End of the Beginning: Assessing the Potential Economic Implications of Prolonged UK-EU Trade Policy Uncertainty*, Santa Monica, Calif.: RAND Corporation, RR-4265-RC, 2020; Bank of England, Monetary Policy Committee, "In Focus: Uncertainty and Brexit," in Bank of England, *Monetary Policy Report*, London, November 2019).

Oxford-AstraZeneca vaccine, it was one of the most aggressive at administering vaccinations once the vaccine was developed. From only 3.37 percent on January 10, 2021, more than half of the UK population (50.02 percent) had received at least one dose by April 27, 2021 (the United States was at 42.38 percent and the EU at 22.65 percent that same date).[20] By August 31, 2021, the UK mark had hit 70.50 percent, well above that of the EU and the United States.[21]

Japan's economic performance in 2020 was far better than that of the EU and the UK but not quite as good as that of the United States. As with most countries, its worst quarter was the second quarter of 2020, when GDP fell by 7.9 percent relative to the first quarter, less than that which occurred in the United States. For the full calendar year, GDP fell by 4.6 percent.[22] As with the EU and the UK, recovery stalled. GDP fell 0.9 percent in the first quarter of 2021 (revised upward from a preliminary estimate of –1.3 percent) relative to the last quarter of 2020. However, second quarter 2020 GDP rose by 0.3 percent, and total seasonally adjusted real GDP was still well below the peak reached in the third quarter of 2019.[23]

Australia followed a similar pattern during 2020 but one that was even more mild than that of Japan. GDP in the second quarter of 2020 fell only 7.0 percent and then increased each of the subsequent two quarters, by 3.6 percent and 3.2 percent, respectively.[24] Estimated GDP change for the

---

[20] Our World in Data, undated; data accessed May 30, 2021.

[21] Our World in Data, undated; data accessed September 1, 2021.

[22] Economic and Social Research Office, Cabinet Office, Government of Japan, "Quarterly Estimates of GDP: April–June 2021 (1st Preliminary)," August 16, 2021b. Earlier estimates showed second quarter 2020 GDP down by 8.1 percent and full year 2020 GDP down by 4.7 percent (Economic and Social Research Office, Cabinet Office, Government of Japan, 2021a).

[23] Economic and Social Research Office, Cabinet Office, Government of Japan, 2021b.

[24] Australian Bureau of Statistics, "Australian National Accounts: National Income, Expenditure and Product; Quarterly Estimates of Key Economic Flows in Australia, Including Gross Domestic Product (GDP), Consumption, Investment, Income and Saving; Reference Period June 2021," September 1, 2021b. The third and fourth quarter 2020 GDP figures were revised upward from 3.4 percent and 3.1 percent, respectively, from earlier estimates (Australian Bureau of Statistics, "Australian National Accounts: National Income, Expenditure and Product; Quarterly Estimates of Key Economic

full year was −2.5 percent.[25] Growth continued into 2021—specifically, 1.9 percent growth in the first quarter and 0.7 percent growth in the second. Calculations based on these growth figures indicate that Australia's seasonally adjusted real GDP was fully restored by the first quarter of 2021, surpassing the previous high in the fourth quarter of 2019.

Australia was able to limit the disease and carry on largely normally, at least economically, because of strict lockdowns and border closures and strong testing and contact tracing.[26] However, the measures Australia has taken are among the most extreme. For example, Australians need government permission to exit the country, and barriers to travel between states have often been instituted. At one point, the chief health officer of one state told residents not to engage in conversation or be friendly to others when they were outside.[27] Given the lockdowns, although the overall economy fared better than most, some service sectors, such as the restaurant industry, suffered. Furthermore, with delays in procuring vaccines and a slow rollout, vaccination rates lagged.[28] For example, as of June 30, 2021, only 23.63 percent of Australians had received at least one dose, compared with 53.72 percent in the United States. By August 31, 2021, Australia's figure had risen markedly to 47.28 percent.[29]

In contrast, India, the fourth member of the Quad, suffered a sizable economic decline in 2020. The second quarter of calendar year 2020 was par-

---

Flows in Australia, Including Gross Domestic Product (GDP), Consumption, Investment, Income and Saving; Reference Period December 2020," March 3, 2021a).

[25] This figure is not official; it is derived from aggregating quarterly totals and applying quarterly growth rates when equivalent quarterly totals were not available because of a change in reference year. Australia does not report changes in calendar year GDP.

[26] Jamie Smyth, "How Australia Brought the Coronavirus Pandemic Under Control," *Financial Times*, November 13, 2020; Frances Mao, "'Fortress Australia': Why Calls to Open Up Borders Are Meeting Resistance," BBC, May 26, 2021; William A. Haseltine, "What Can We Learn from Australia's COVID-19 Response?" *Forbes*, March 24, 2021.

[27] James Morrow, "Covid Mania Returns Australia to Its Roots as a Nation of Prisoners," *Wall Street Journal*, July 25, 2021.

[28] Michael E. Miller, "Australia, Once a Pandemic Hero, Now Struggles with Vaccination," *Washington Post*, July 18, 2021, p. A20.

[29] Our World in Data, undated; data accessed September 1, 2021.

ticularly bad, with GDP falling 24.4 percent relative to the second quarter of calendar year 2019.[30] For the full calendar year, GDP fell by 6.9 percent, worse than the United States and Japan but not as bad as the EU or the UK. In addition, the quarter beginning October 2020 and the quarter beginning January 2021 both showed growth from the same periods in 2019 and 2020, although they remained well below the growth rates of previous years.[31]

India provides a cautionary illustration of the great uncertainty surrounding the course of the pandemic. India had appeared to get the disease under control by November 2020. Then, starting in late March 2021, cases surged from the delta variant, which first emerged in India in December 2020.[32] From 11.41 million confirmed cases as of March 15, 2021, the number of confirmed cases had shot up to 28.81 million by May 31, 2021. Confirmed deaths rose from 159,000 to almost 331,895 in the same period.[33] Confirmed cases soon leveled off, but confirmed deaths continued to rise rapidly through the end of June 2021, when they hit 399,459 on June 30, 2021.

Whereas the 2020 cases had largely affected poorer people, the new surge affected people of all socioeconomic levels. Although the wave had peaked by late May or early June 2021 (with significant variation by

---

[30] India's official statistics are recorded on a financial year basis, and each year starts in April. So in the India data, this is the change from 2020 to 2021 first quarter data. The sequential change from first quarter calendar year 2020 to second quarter calendar year 2020 was –29.6 percent, but it is not clear that the official data are seasonally adjusted. So, this might not be comparable to the sequential data provided for other countries in this report. See Ministry of Statistics and Programme Implementation, Government of India, "Annual and Quarterly Estimates of GDP at Constant Prices (2011-12 Series)," Excel spreadsheet, March 5, 2021a.

[31] Ministry of Statistics and Programme Implementation, Government of India, "Annual and Quarterly Estimates of GDP at Constant Prices (2011-12 Series)," Excel spreadsheet, June 1, 2021b. GDP in the quarter beginning January 2021 was higher than all preceding quarterly GDP figures, but because it does not appear that the data are seasonally adjusted, it is not possible to say that India had fully recovered by early 2021. Even if it had, the emergence of the delta variant, as discussed in the text, likely resulted in GDP decline in the quarter beginning March 2021.

[32] Meredith Wadman, "What Does the Delta Variant Have in Store for the United States? We Asked Coronavirus Experts," *Science*, August 4, 2021.

[33] Our World in Data, undated; data accessed September 1, 2021.

states), the recurrence served as a warning that uncertainties remain with the course of the pandemic.[34] As well, India embarked on a more aggressive vaccination drive. Although only 0.89 percent of the population had received at least one shot as of March 1, 2021, that number had risen to 35.67 percent as of August 31, 2021.[35] Notably, the delta variant had surged worldwide by the summer, again serving as a warning that even countries that had initially controlled the disease could be at risk from new forms of the virus.[36]

Conclusion

Most U.S. allies and partners faced large economic slowdowns in 2020 because of the pandemic. The EU and Japan experienced further negative growth in early 2021, and India was slammed by a surge that left the country reeling. Missteps in the UK resulted in high levels of deaths and a dramatic slowdown, and missteps in the EU resulted in a slow initial vaccine rollout.

Except for India, which had been experiencing rapid economic growth, COVID-19 extended existing trends. Slow growth in the EU and Japan has been ongoing, and their economic weight in the world has been receding. But two notable developments could represent bright spots for the future. First, the large EU bond issuance could end up strengthening EU economies. Second, as will be discussed in Chapter Seven, the Quad countries agreed to an ambitious vaccine distribution plan that could speed global recovery and show the value of alliance cooperation.

---

[34] Soutik Biswas, "COVID-19: Has India's Deadly Second Wave Peaked?" BBC, May 26, 2021; Antonia Noori Farzan and Claire Parker, "How Did the COVID-19 Outbreak in India Get So Bad?" *Washington Post*, April 28, 2021.

[35] Our World in Data, undated; data accessed September 1, 2021.

[36] Roshan Abraham and Kavya B., "Global COVID-19 Cases Surpass 200 Mln as Delta Variant Spreads," Reuters, August 4, 2021.

CHAPTER SIX

The Developing World

As a group, the developing economies did not perform poorly in 2020 relative to the rest of the world; their GDP fell by only 2.1 percent. In fact, it even appeared initially that parts of the developing world, such as sub-Saharan Africa, were experiencing only limited effects on public health compared with the rest of the world.[1] In that region, GDP fell by only 1.8 percent.[2]

But the aggregate economic consequences mask tremendous variation within the developing world. The small GDP loss was driven in part by China's positive performance and by growth in some parts of Africa. GDP fell by 7.0 percent in Latin America and the Caribbean and by 3.4 percent in the Middle East and North Africa.[3]

Furthermore, economic trends have taken a more dire turn, driven in large part by limited distribution of effective vaccines. In its July 2021 outlook, the IMF lowered its 2021 growth projections relative to figures in its April 2021 outlook for emerging market and developing economies overall, driven by lower projections for emerging and developing Asia, especially India, and for low-income developing countries as a group. Growth is still projected to be high—up 6.3 percent in 2021 and 5.2 percent in 2022 for emerging market and developing economies overall, and 3.9 percent in 2021

---

[1] Michael Shurkin, Alexander Noyes, and Mary Kate Adgie, *The COVID-19 Pandemic in Sub-Saharan Africa: An Opportunity to Rethink Strategic Competition on the Continent*, Santa Monica, Calif.: RAND Corporation, PE-A1055-1, 2021.

[2] IMF, 2021d. These figures are slight upward revisions from earlier estimates of –2.2 percent and –1.9 percent (IMF, 2021b, p. 39).

[3] IMF, 2021b, pp. 37–38.

and 5.5 percent in 2022 for low-income developing economies as a group—but the risks of lowering projections further are also high.[4]

The Developing World in the Geoeconomic Balance

The economic performance of the developing world is important for several reasons. From the perspective of self-interest of the advanced economies, the developing world contributes to global growth and the growth of advanced countries. One analysis found that excluding most middle- and low-income countries from vaccine distribution would reduce annual global GDP by more than $1.2 trillion, and almost 40 percent of these losses would occur in the EU, the United States, and the UK.[5]

As a concrete example, in August 2021, the spread of the delta variant throughout Asia disrupted supply chains for goods meant for the United States.[6] The pandemic caused some factories to be shut down and others to reduce operations, cutting supply to such Western companies as Adidas, a German shoe company, and Crocs, an American shoe company. The slow-down in Vietnam inspired Nike, an American shoe company, and Gap, an American apparel company, among many other companies, to ask President Biden to speed vaccine donations there.

A second, related reason for the importance of the economic performance of developing countries is that the pandemic induced dramatic increases in global poverty. The number of people living in extreme poverty—that is, those living on less than $1.90 per day—is estimated to have risen from 655 million in 2019 to 732 million in 2020 and was pro-

---

[4] IMF, 2021d.

[5] Marco Hafner, Erez Yerushalmi, Clement Fays, Elaine Dufresne, and Christian van Stolk, *COVID-19 and the Cost of Vaccine Nationalism*, Santa Monica, Calif., and Cambridge, UK: RAND Corporation, RR-A769-1, 2020.

[6] Jon Emont and Lam Le, "Delta Variant Outbreaks in Sparsely Vaccinated Asian Countries Disrupt Production," *Wall Street Journal*, August 25, 2021.

jected to stay elevated at 711 million in 2021.[7] The consequences have been dire for some. The United Nations Food and Agricultural Organization estimated that the number of people undernourished rose from 650.3 million in 2019 to 768 million in 2020, and the share of the world's population suffering undernourishment rose from 8.4 percent to 9.9 percent.[8] This not only reduces global goals of poverty reduction and increases human suffering but also hampers the ability of countries to grow and contribute to the world economy. Social and political strife might also increase, further hampering economic progress.

A final reason for the importance of the economic performance of developing countries is that they provide the principal terrain in which great power competition plays out. For example, China and Russia both tried to use the COVID-19 pandemic to increase their influence in sub-Saharan Africa but with little evidence of success, at least during the first year of the pandemic.[9] Furthermore, nearly all inter- and intrastate conflicts since World War II have taken place in the developing world. And COVID-19 seems likely to have an even greater effect on these societies than on major powers.

The developed world spent little more than a year fully exposed to COVID-19 before the advent of vaccines and might spend two more years so exposed, twice as long as the economically advanced countries, before achieving significant vaccination rates. The pressures on economic and social well-being could lead to increases in state failure, civil wars, extremist movements, and migration, all of which can affect the global competition among the major powers. These threats provide greater incentive for the advanced countries to ensure widespread distribution of vaccines.

---

[7] Daniel Gerszon Mahler, Nishant Yonzan, Christoph Lakner, R. Andres Castaneda Aguilar, and Haoyu Wu, "Updated Estimates of the Impact of COVID-19 on Global Poverty: Turning the Corner on the Pandemic in 2021?" *Data Blog*, World Bank, June 24, 2021.

[8] Food and Agricultural Organization of the United Nations, "Hunger and Food Insecurity," webpage, undated. The 2020 figure is estimated with a range of 720.4 million to 811 million and 9.2 percent to 10.4 percent.

[9] Shurkin, Noyes, and Adgie, 2021, p. 12.

Consequences of COVID-19 in the Developing World

As noted at the beginning of this chapter, the average economic performance of the developing world in 2020—a GDP decline of only 2.1 percent—masks tremendous variation:

- In emerging and developing Europe, the average GDP decline was 2.0 percent, but outcomes ranged from a 9.0 percent decline in Croatia to a 1.8 percent increase in Turkey.[10]
- In emerging and developing Asia, the average GDP decline was 1.0 percent (driven in large part by China's growth), but outcomes ranged from a 9.5 percent decline in the Philippines to a 2.9 percent increase in Vietnam.[11]
- In emerging and developing Latin America and the Caribbean, the average GDP decline was 7.0 percent, making it the worst-performing region. All economies for which data are provided experienced declines, some quite sizable: Argentina down 10.0 percent, Peru down 11.1 percent, and Venezuela down 30.0 percent.[12]
- Finally, in emerging and developing Middle East and Central Asia, the average GDP decline was 2.0 percent. Outcomes ranged from an increase of 3.6 percent in Egypt to declines of 10.0 percent in Iraq and 25.0 percent in Lebanon, although the Lebanon decline was sparked by factors beyond COVID-19, including an explosion at the main port in Beirut and a financial and currency crisis.[13]

Developing economies as a group are expected to perform well through 2022. Growth of 6.3 percent is expected in 2021 and 5.2 percent in 2022.[14] Asia is expected to perform best at 7.5 percent growth—although not as well

---

[10] IMF, 2021b, p. 35.

[11] IMF, 2021b, p. 36.

[12] IMF, 2021b, pp. 8, 37.

[13] IMF, 2021b, pp. 8, 38.

[14] IMF, 2021d, p. 6.

as projected earlier in 2021—followed by Latin America and the Caribbean's strong rebound of 5.8 percent.

However, the developing regions will face long-term challenges and heightened risks as long as vaccination rates remain lower than in advanced countries and especially as countries wrestle with the delta variant.[15] Responses to the pandemic kept about 1.6 billion children out of school in 2020, and this carries long-term consequences for human capital formation and economic growth.[16] Inequality across several dimensions, including access to health and jobs, has also widened and might remain widened over several years.

In response to the ongoing pandemic-induced economic difficulties, international organizations have increased assistance through a variety of mechanisms. As of late August 2021, one of the latest was the largest allocation of the IMF reserve asset, known as *special drawing rights*, in the organization's history. Valued at $650 billion, the allocation came into effect on August 23, 2021, to provide $275 billion to emerging and developing countries, of which $21 billion was to go to low-income countries. In some cases, this would equal about 6 percent of their GDP, similar to the sizable fiscal programs instituted by economically advanced countries.[17]

Conclusion

As of late summer 2021, access to vaccines was improving, though unevenly. As of August 31, 2021, the percentage of people who had received at least one dose was 64.56 in the EU, 60.96 in the United States, and 54.53 in South America. However, only 5.01 percent of people in Africa had received one

---

[15] Gabriele Steinhauser and Joe Parkinson, "Third Covid Wave Upends Fragile South Africa, a Warning for the Developing World," *Wall Street Journal*, July 19, 2021; Jon Emont, "Covid-19 Deaths Rise Sharply in Indonesia," *Wall Street Journal*, July 27, 2021.

[16] Organisation for Economic Co-operation and Development, *Perspectives on Global Development 2021: From Protest to Progress?* Paris: OECD Publishing, 2021, p. 27.

[17] IMF, "IMF Managing Director Announces the US$650 Billion SDR Allocation Comes into Effect," press release, Washington, D.C., August 23, 2021e.

dose.[18] Distribution slowed during the late spring and summer of 2021 in part because of the surge of COVID-19 in India and a concomitant reduction of vaccine supply from that country, as discussed in Chapter Seven. It was also due to the inability of some countries to develop vaccines despite promising to supply them and to developed economies wanting to ensure the health of their own populations first, thus reserving supply for themselves.[19]

The developing world has been the primary field for geopolitical competition. China and Russia have been active in at least getting high levels of notice that they are willing to distribute their vaccines worldwide. The reality is a bit more distant from the pronouncements. Take Latin America as an example. As of mid-May 2021, China had delivered only limited quantities, and those had been sold rather than donated. Russia had run into delays because of temporary production and logistics problems.[20] But the United States had also been largely absent, despite the fact that assisting with vaccine distribution would provide a "cost effective way to strengthen goodwill and cooperative relationships" with a neighboring region.[21] Thanks to new media and social media, it is easy to see that at least some residents in developing countries know that their regions are in play. They also know the difference between statements and action.[22]

---

[18] Our World in Data, undated; data accessed September 1, 2021.

[19] Gabriele Steinhauser, Drew Hinshaw, and Betsy McKay, "Why a Grand Plan to Vaccinate the World Against COVID Unraveled," *Wall Street Journal*, May 26, 2021.

[20] R. Evan Ellis, "A Race Against Time: Deploying Vaccines and Addressing the Disproportionate Impacts of Covid-19 in Latin America and the Caribbean," testimony presented before the U.S. House of Representatives Subcommittee on the Western Hemisphere, Civilian Security, Migration, and International Economic Policy, Washington, D.C., May 13, 2021.

[21] Ellis, 2021, p. 5.

[22] For some pointed comments in this vein, see the Twitter feed (tweets, retweets, and replies) of the Nigerian who goes by Onye Nkuzi (*teacher* or *instructor* in Igbo) at the handle @cchukudebelu. For example, one tweet from March 7, 2021, said, "There's a 'great power competition to finance infrastructure in Africa' in the tweets of Western geopolitical analysts, in Western newspapers & in policy briefs by Western think tanks. In real life, Africa's $130 - 170 billion/year infrastructure deficit, is far from being met" (Onye Nkuzi [@cchukudebelu], "There's a 'great power competition to finance infrastructure in Africa' in the tweets of Western geopolitical analysts," Twitter post, March 7, 2021).

But there are more-important implications than geopolitical competition. The primary implications are for the well-being of the residents of developing countries, spillovers to the more economically advanced countries, and the recovery of the global economy. The pandemic is unlikely to fully end unless large proportions of the population in developing countries are vaccinated. Vaccinating these populations will not only save lives but also allow these economies to recover, enhance trade prospects, and reduce the risk of new, more-dangerous variants emerging.[23]

---

[23] David Malpass, "How to Vaccinate Every Country," *Voices: Perspectives on Development*, blog, World Bank, May 27, 2021. Malpass is the president of the World Bank.

CHAPTER SEVEN

Vaccine Diplomacy

With the 2017 *National Security Strategy*, the Trump administration high-lighted the idea that the world is a setting for competition among nations, shifting the United States from a nearly two-decade focus on countering nonstate armed groups.[1] The Biden administration built on this theme with its *Interim National Security Strategic Guidance*, released in March 2021.[2] The 2017 document focused on China and Russia as the United States' leading competitors; the 2021 document acknowledged the challenge of Russia but focused more specifically on China.

The COVID-19 pandemic showed that global competition is adaptive and can extend to areas far beyond traditional security and economic competition. Specifically, China and Russia early in the pandemic made clear that they would serve the needs of the global public and widely distribute any vaccines they developed, a phenomenon that has come to be known as *vaccine diplomacy*. In contrast, the United States, despite Operation Warp Speed, held back in 2020 from any promises of global distribution—although that changed in 2021.

The need for global distribution was recognized very early. Leaving large parts of the world without vaccines would extract a large human cost in terms of death and disease, raise the risk of new variants developing that might negate the benefits of vaccination, and damage the global economy.

The idea for some kind of multilateral distribution facility first emerged in January 2020. Soon after, three organizations—Gavi, the Vaccine Alli-

---

[1] White House, *National Security Strategy of the United States*, Washington, D.C., December 2017.

[2] White House, *Interim National Security Strategic Guidance*, Washington, D.C., March 2021b.

ance; the Coalition for Epidemic Preparedness Innovations; and the World Health Organization—formed the COVID-19 Vaccines Global Access (COVAX) Facility. The EU countries became prominent backers, and the Serum Institute of India became the main supplier. China, Russia, and the United States did not participate in the early stages.[3] Originally envisioned as a way to distribute vaccines globally, it has evolved into an international alliance to ensure the distribution of vaccines to lower-income countries.

COVAX has not quite worked as hoped, although by the late summer of 2021, it had started to accelerate vaccine distribution. More than 230 million doses had been distributed to more than 139 countries as of August 31, 2021.[4] Western countries opted to focus on their own populations, while China and Russia opted to distribute vaccines largely on their own. Both countries have been using vaccine diplomacy to shore up their images. And although they are fulfilling a desperate global need, they also both face risks if their vaccines turn out not to be as efficacious as promised. As of spring 2021, the United States and its allied partners have started to turn their attention to vaccine distribution using highly effective, Western-developed vaccines. This chapter discusses vaccine diplomacy by the United States, China, Russia, and U.S. allies and partners and the geopolitical implications.

The United States

During 2020, to the surprise of many, an innovative industrial policy program called Operation Warp Speed supported the rapid creation of vaccines for COVID-19, and these vaccines started to be administered in late 2020. As a consequence, the United States was one of the world leaders in vaccinating its own population. The United States has lagged, however, in the international distribution of COVID-19 vaccines; as of May 2021, its efforts had been smaller and lower-profile than those of China and Russia.

---

[3] Steinhauser, Hinshaw, and McKay, 2021.

[4] Gavi, the Vaccine Alliance, "COVAX Vaccine Roll-Out: Country Updates," webpage, last updated August 31, 2021b.

The United States pledged $1.16 billion for Gavi, the Vaccine Alliance, at the Global Vaccine Summit in June 2020.[5] This was not directed at COVAX, however. U.S. legislation in December 2020 allocated $4 billion to Gavi. The Biden administration then announced that it would allocate $2 billion of that for COVAX and would release an additional $2 billion through 2022.[6] Congress then allocated more than $11 billion for global COVID-19 response—not just for vaccine distribution—and the administration named a coordinator for global COVID-19 response.[7] And working with Japan, Australia, and India as the Quad, the United States pledged to support the production of 1 billion doses through the end of 2022, along with various joint activities.[8]

Despite these moves, the United States had also been slow at distributing vaccines that it had on hand but was unlikely to use. Specifically, the United States held 60 million doses of the AstraZeneca vaccine, which had not been given emergency use authorization by the U.S. Food and Drug Administration but which had been approved for use by the UK in December 2020, the EU in January 2021, and the World Health Organization in February 2021. This left the United States open to the charge of hoarding these vaccines; in early March 2021, more than 70 countries had approved the vaccine, yet the United States had denied requests to lend U.S. doses abroad.[9] Finally, later in March 2021, the White House agreed to lend 4 million doses combined to Mexico and Canada and by late April 2021 said it would be sending the remaining doses abroad in May and June 2021.[10]

---

[5] Gavi, the Vaccine Alliance, "Donor Profiles," webpage, last updated March 31, 2021a.

[6] White House, "Fact Sheet: President Biden to Take Action on Global Health Through Support of COVAX and Calling for Health Security Financing," February 18, 2021a.

[7] U.S. Department of State, "Secretary Antony J. Blinken Remarks to the Press on the COVID Response," briefing, April 5, 2021a.

[8] White House, "Fact Sheet: Quad Summit," March 12, 2021c.

[9] Noah Weiland and Rebecca Robbins, "The U.S. Is Sitting on Tens of Millions of Vaccine Doses the World Needs," *New York Times*, March 11, 2021.

[10] White House, "Press Briefing by White House COVID-19 Response Team and Public Health Officials," Washington, D.C., March 19, 2021e; Colm Quinn, "U.S. Announces Plans to Export Its AstraZeneca Vaccine Stockpile," *Foreign Policy*, April 27, 2021.

In a separate move, U.S. Trade Representative Katherine Tai announced in early May 2021 that the United States would be willing to waive patent protections for COVID-19 vaccines as a means of boosting production.[11] This will require agreement within the World Trade Organization, and negotiations are likely to be protracted. Several major trading partners and allies of the United States, particularly France and Germany, have objected. Furthermore, patents do not appear to be the main constraint on production and distribution, so it is not clear that this move will accelerate global vaccine distribution.[12]

U.S. attention toward international vaccine distribution started to shift in May 2021, when the United States announced that it would distribute 80 million doses by the end of June 2021, including the 60 million AstraZeneca doses.[13] In early June 2021, it laid out further plans for doing so. Twenty-five percent of the total doses were to be made available for immediate use for surges around the world, and 75 percent (60 million doses) would go to COVAX. Concrete plans for the first 25 million doses were outlined, and 19 million doses were going to COVAX.[14]

In June 2021, the G-7 countries agreed at the annual summit meeting to provide 1 billion doses worldwide. The United States committed to provide half of that amount, 500 million doses, through COVAX.[15] And the next month, the White House released a framework for the U.S. COVID-19

---

[11] Office of the U.S. Trade Representative, "Statement from Ambassador Katherine Tai on the COVID-19 Trips Waiver," Washington, D.C., May 5, 2021.

[12] Krishna Kumar, "Vaccine Patents Debate Risks Becoming a Sideshow in the Global Battle Against COVID-19," *The Hill*, May 16, 2021b.

[13] White House, "Biden-Harris Administration Is Providing at Least 80 Million COVID-19 Vaccines for Global Use, Commits to Leading a Multilateral Effort Toward Ending the Pandemic," fact sheet, May 17, 2021f.

[14] White House, "Biden-Harris Administration Unveils Strategy for Global Vaccine Sharing, Announcing Allocation Plan for the First 25 Million Doses to Be Shared Globally," fact sheet, June 3, 2021g.

[15] White House, "United States and G7+ Plan to Defeat the COVID-19 Pandemic in 2022 and Prevent the Next Pandemic," fact sheet, June 11, 2021h.

global response.[16] By August 27, 2021, the United States had distributed almost 128 million doses, mostly through COVAX, to more than 80 countries.[17] U.S. officials noted in September 2021 that the United States had donated more doses than all other countries combined.[18]

China

In the scramble to develop, purchase, and distribute vaccines for COVID-19, developing countries have been at the end of the line. In response, China has actively sought to partner with other countries to distribute the vaccines it has developed and even manufacture them abroad to increase supply. As of August 30, 2021, China had delivered 693 million vaccine doses, primarily those developed by Sinovac and Sinopharm, to 106 countries.[19] Of this total, 52 million doses were donated. In addition, in early May 2021, the World Health Organization gave emergency approval to the use of the Sinopharm vaccine, the first approval for a non-Western vaccine; the other approved vaccines were those developed by Pfizer-BioNTech, Oxford-AstraZeneca, Janssen–Johnson and Johnson, and Moderna.[20] The World Health Organization then gave approval on June 1, 2021, to the Sinovac vaccine.[21]

China has positioned this as part of its broader efforts at building partnerships, particularly through its Belt and Road Initiative. At his Boao

---

[16] White House, *U.S. COVID-19 Global Response and Recovery Framework*, Washington, D.C., July 1, 2021i.

[17] U.S. Department of State, "COVID-19 Vaccine Donations," webpage, data last updated August 27, 2021b.

[18] White House, "Press Briefing by White House COVID-19 Response Team and Public Health Officials," Washington, D.C., September 2, 2021j.

[19] Bridge, "China COVID-19 Vaccine Tracker," last updated August 30, 2021.

[20] "Sinopharm: Chinese Covid Vaccine Gets WHO Emergency Approval," BBC, May 7, 2021. The World Health Organization gave emergency use authorization to the Covishield vaccine produced by the Serum Institute of India, an Oxford-AstraZeneca formulation, on February 15, 2021 (World Health Organization, "WHO Lists Two Additional COVID-19 Vaccines for Emergency Use and COVAX Roll-Out," news release, Geneva, Switzerland, February 15, 2021a).

[21] "Covid: China's Sinovac Vaccine Gets WHO Emergency Approval," BBC, June 2, 2021.

Forum speech in April 2021, Chinese leader Xi Jinping said that his country would build "a closer partnership for health cooperation" as part of high-quality Belt and Road cooperation.[22] This would include cooperation on infectious disease control, public health, and traditional medicine, among other areas. In addition, "China will continue to carry out anti-COVID cooperation with the WHO [World Health Organization] and other countries, honor its commitment of making vaccines a global public good, and do more to help developing countries defeat the virus."[23]

Although distribution of the vaccines has the potential to dramatically improve public health and improve China's image, available data indicate that several of the Chinese vaccines are less effective than the Western vaccines.[24] This has had two results. First, positive effects that are population-wide will take longer, and disease resurgences could occur.[25] Second, although the Chinese vaccines used require two shots, countries have started to consider the need for a third, booster shot.[26] These results, combined with a lack of transparency about vaccine trials, particularly a failure to publish results in peer-reviewed journals, have resulted in a drop in confidence in the vaccines.[27] This might be a temporary situation. Given the rapidly evolving nature of the pandemic, vaccine efficacy, and future actions, it is not possible to determine the ultimate consequences of China's vaccine diplomacy, although it is clear that China is putting significant effort into sharing its vaccines worldwide.

---

[22] Xi Jinping, "Pulling Together Through Adversity and Toward a Shared Future for All," keynote speech delivered at the Boao Forum for Asia Annual Conference 2021, Boao, China, April 20, 2021, p. 4.

[23] Xi Jinping, 2021, p. 5.

[24] Fabian Schmidt, "Coronavirus: How Effective Are the Chinese Vaccines?" DW, February 1, 2021.

[25] Ryan Dube, "First Dose of Chinese Covid-19 Vaccine Offers Little Protection, Chile Learns," *Wall Street Journal*, April 18, 2021.

[26] Isabel Debre, "UAE to Offer Booster Shot to Recipients of Sinopharm Vaccine," Associated Press, May 18, 2021.

[27] Eva Dou and Shibani Mahtani, "China's Vaccine Diplomacy Stumbles as Clinical Trial Data Remains Absent," *Washington Post*, March 23, 2021.

Russia

Like many scientifically advanced countries, Russia embarked on its own vaccine development to counter COVID-19. As of April 2021, the country had three vaccines.[28] The most prominent of these is known as the Sputnik V, developed by the Gamaleya National Research Center of Epidemiology and Microbiology and found to have strong efficacy against COVID-19.[29] As of August 31, 2021, 45 countries were using the vaccine, and the vaccine had been approved in at least 70 countries.[30] Russia had also arranged for its manufacture abroad—for example, in Italy and India.[31] In addition, Russia has been working to get the vaccine included in multilateral efforts designed to bring vaccines to lower-income countries. As of late May 2021, the Russian Direct Investment Fund had agreed to supply doses sufficient for 110 million people to the United Nations Children's Fund and was in talks with Gavi, the Vaccine Alliance, to get the Sputnik V included in COVAX.[32]

Despite these achievements, doubts have been raised about the vaccine's safety and the trial results. In Europe, Hungary and Slovakia approved the vaccine, but as of late May 2021, the European Medicines Agency had not authorized its use.[33] In late April 2021, Brazil declined to authorize the use

---

[28] Putin, 2021.

[29] Ian Jones and Polly Roy, "Sputnik V COVID-19 Vaccine Candidate Appears Safe and Effective," *The Lancet*, Vol. 397, No. 10275, February 20, 2021. In May, Russia approved a one-dose version, Sputnik Light (Russian Direct Investment Fund, "Single Dose Vaccine, Sputnik Light, Authorized for Use in Russia," press release, Moscow, May 6, 2021a).

[30] Josh Holder, "Tracking Coronavirus Vaccinations Around the World," *New York Times*, last updated September 3, 2021; Russian Direct Investment Fund, "Indonesia Becomes the 70th Country to Approve the Sputnik V Vaccine," press release, Moscow, August 25, 2021d.

[31] Colleen Barry and Daria Litvinova, "Russia to Make Sputnik V Vaccine in Italy, a First in EU," Associated Press, March 9, 2021; Russian Direct Investment Fund, "RDIF and Panacea Biotec Launch the Production of Sputnik V in India," press release, Moscow, May 24, 2021b.

[32] Russian Direct Investment Fund, "RDIF and UNICEF Sign Sputnik V Vaccine Supply Agreement," press release, Moscow, May 27, 2021c.

[33] "Slovakia Becomes 2nd EU Country to Approve Russia's Sputnik," Associated Press, May 26, 2021. Notably, in early April 2021, Slovakia had rejected a batch of Sputnik V,

of Sputnik V, citing quality and safety issues.[34] As of May 2021, the biggest problem seemed to be questions about transparency of and access to data from vaccine testing.[35] Accordingly, countries might learn the vaccine's efficacy only after its large-scale use. Notably, a study in St. Petersburg in July and August 2021 found Sputnik V to be effective against the delta variant.[36] However, as of August 19, 2021, Sputnik V had still not received emergency use authorization from the World Health Organization, pending submission of data and a follow-up inspection.[37]

Europe, the United Kingdom, and the Quad Countries

Early in the pandemic, the EU took a strong stance toward global cooperation, with the leaders of France, Germany, and the World Health Organization in April 2020 announcing an $8 billion funding drive.[38] The European

---

saying it was different from the version that had high efficacy (Karel Janicek, "Russia Wants Slovakia to Return Its Sputnik V Vaccines," Associated Press, April 8, 2021). Apparently, by late May 2021, these disagreements had been resolved.

[34] Sofia Moutinho and Meredith Wadman, "Is Russia's COVID-19 Vaccine Safe? Brazil's Veto of Sputnik V Sparks Lawsuit Threat and Confusion," *Science*, April 30, 2021.

[35] Enrico M. Bucci, Johannes Berkhof, André Gillibert, Gowri Gopalakrishna, Raffaele A. Calogero, and Lex M. Bouter, "Data Discrepancies and Substandard Reporting of Interim Data of Sputnik V Phase 3 Trial," *The Lancet*, Vol. 397, No. 10288, May 22, 2021; Jonathan Cushing, "Is the Sputnik V Vaccine Too Good to Be True? Without the Data, It's Hard to Know," Stat, May 26, 2021.

[36] Anton Barchuk, Mikhail Cherkashin, Anna Bulina, Natalia Berezina, Tatyana Rakova, Darya Kuplevatskaya, Oksana Stanevich, Dmitriy Skougarevskiy, and Artemiy Okhotin, "Vaccine Effectiveness Against Referral to Hospital and Severe Lung Injury Associated with COVID-19: A Population-Based Case-Control Study in St. Petersburg, Russia," MedRxiv, Preprint Server for Health Sciences, August 25, 2021; Olga Dobrovidova, "Russia's Sputnik V Protects Against Severe COVID-19 from Delta Variant, Study Shows," *Science*, August 26, 2021.

[37] World Health Organization, "Status of COVID-19 Vaccines Within WHO EUL/PQ Evaluation Process," guidance document, August 19, 2021b.

[38] Hugo Miller and Ania Nussbaum, "Merkel, Macron Back $8 Billion Virus Vaccine Fund Effort," *Bloomberg*, April 24, 2020.

Commission and member states have also been strong contributors to the COVAX funding stream that supports the distribution of vaccines to low- and middle-income countries, with Germany alone committing more than $1 billion to this effort for the 2021 to 2025 period (for the same period, the European Commission committed $472 million, France committed $118 million, and Italy committed $103 million).[39]

However, as with the United States—but in contrast to China and Russia—the EU's role in the global distribution of vaccines got off to a slow start. This is likely largely because of the delay in vaccinating EU residents. This pace shifted with a late-May 2021 meeting of the European Council. The EU heads of state committed to accelerate the distribution of vaccines and set a goal of distributing at least 100 million doses abroad and helping develop local manufacturing capacity.[40] By July 2021, the EU institutions and member states had pledged to donate 200 million doses by the end of 2021.[41] Germany, France, and Italy were also part of the G-7's commitment to donate 1 billion doses. Despite this commitment, the effort was still stumbling in August 2021, when the EU had donated only 7.9 million doses by August 2, 2021.[42]

The UK has committed $446.1 million to Gavi COVID-19 efforts for the 2021 to 2025 period, and Japan has committed $160 million to the Gavi COVID-19 vaccine effort.[43] Both countries were part of the G-7 commitment. In late July 2021, the UK had started distributing 9 million doses.[44] In

---

[39] Gavi, the Vaccine Alliance, 2021a. The fund to which they contributed is the COVID-19 Vaccines Advance Market Commitment.

[40] European Council, General Secretariat of the Council, "Special Meeting of the European Council (24 and 25 May 2021)—Conclusions," note to delegations, Brussels, May 25, 2021.

[41] European Commission, "Vaccinating the World: 'Team Europe' to Share More than 200 Million Doses of COVID-19 Vaccines with Low and Middle-Income Countries, by the End of 2021," press release, Brussels, July 22, 2021.

[42] Jillian Deutsch and Ashleigh Furlong, "EU Falls Behind China, US on Vaccine Donations: Document," *Politico*, August 2, 2021.

[43] Gavi, the Vaccine Alliance, 2021a.

[44] Government of the United Kingdom, "UK Begins Donating Millions of COVID-19 Vaccines Overseas," press release, London, July 28, 2021.

addition, Japan and Australia played an important role in the Quad's March 2021 actions related to COVID-19 vaccines.

Among all U.S. allies and partners, India has been by far the most prominent in carrying out vaccine diplomacy under the auspices of the Vaccine Matri, or Vaccine Friendship, Initiative.[45] Despite less of a public relations pitch, this effort appeared to be outstripping that of Russia and China, at least until the end of March 2021, when the COVID-19 surge hit India itself. India's experience illustrates the ongoing uncertainty regarding the effects of the pandemic.

India is the third-largest producer of pharmaceuticals in the world and as of March 2021 was producing two different vaccines—the Oxford-AstraZeneca vaccine and one developed in India, called Covaxin.[46] Although approved in some countries, Covaxin had not yet been approved by the World Health Organization as of August 2021.[47]

By May 29, 2021, India had distributed more than 66 million doses to 95 countries.[48] Of these doses, 11 million were grants, 36 million were delivered on a commercial basis, and 20 million were delivered under the COVAX Facility to poor countries.[49]

However, as with much else in India, the coronavirus surge has upended this activity. India suspended vaccine exports in late March 2021 to focus on immunizing its own population.[50] The Serum Institute of India, the main manufacturer of vaccines for COVAX, said it would be unable to provide

---

[45] Mandakini D. Surie, "India's Vaccine Diplomacy: Made in India, Shared with the World," *DevPolicy Blog*, March 29, 2021.

[46] Surie, 2021.

[47] World Health Organization, 2021b; "COVID Vaccines: Without WHO Approval, Covaxin Remains Second Among Equals," The Wire, May 25, 2021.

[48] Ministry of External Affairs, Government of India, "Vaccine Supply: Made-in-India COVID-19 Vaccine Supplies So Far (in Lakhs)," COVID-19 Updates, webpage, last updated May 29, 2021. As of September 3, 2021, the webpage with this information had not been updated beyond May 29, 2021.

[49] Numbers do not add to 66 million because of rounding.

[50] Rajesh Roy and Vibhuti Agarwal, "India Suspends COVID-19 Vaccine Exports to Focus on Domestic Immunization," *Wall Street Journal*, March 25, 2021.

new doses potentially until the end of 2021.[51] This left COVAX and countries relying on it to seek new supplies of the vaccine.

Conclusion

Ensuring global access to COVID-19 vaccines is important to global economic recovery. Societies where the disease is under control are better able to maintain domestic goods and service production and international transactions involving any face-to-face dealings. This is especially important for the tourism-dependent economies of Southern Europe, the Caribbean, and elsewhere. Accordingly, vaccine distribution is part of the COVID-19-related economic story.

The experience with vaccine diplomacy shows how any field is open to geopolitical competition and major countries will try to gain advantage where they can. The EU was initially standing strongly behind a multilateral effort. China and Russia were moving independently to meet global demand. The United States in 2020 was focusing on domestic needs first. That has been changing in 2021, but the United States has continued to prioritize domestic vaccinations.

But *succeeding* at geopolitical competition is not so easy. True, as of late August 2021, China had reportedly distributed 693 million doses globally (52 million donated), and the United States had donated 128 million doses. However, the efficacy of China's vaccines appears to be poor compared with the Western alternatives, and vaccination programs using the Chinese vaccine have been associated with further outbreaks, while the Western vaccines appear to be of higher quality. Competition by other countries and areas has also turned out differently from what was hoped. India's forward-thinking program to become the main supplier to COVAX foundered, at least temporarily, on India's domestic needs. And although the EU has supplied money to COVAX, COVAX has had to actually procure vaccines, and

---

[51] Michael Peel, David Pilling, and Stephanie Findlay, "Covax Scrambles to Make Up Vaccine Shortfall Due to Indian Export Halt," *Financial Times*, May 21, 2021.

there the Europeans had fallen short through early August 2021. Russia has also met with resistance and disappointment in a variety of countries.[52]

Even as the pandemic stretched into the second half of its second year, it was too early to evaluate the consequences of vaccine diplomacy. But with their own vaccination rates rising, the efficacy of their vaccines, and their pharmaceutical manufacturing capacity, the United States and its allies, working as a group or through COVAX, appeared to have recovered momentum in expanding high-quality vaccine supply to the world, thereby enhancing the reputation of Western technology, production capacity, and generosity.

---

[52] Anton Mardasov, "Kremlin's Vaccine Diplomacy Finds Trouble in Middle East," *Al-Monitor*, July 16, 2021.

CHAPTER EIGHT

COVID-19, the Global Economy, and Global Competition

The COVID-19 pandemic has unleashed utopian and dystopian visions of the future. On the one hand is the idea of a "Great Reset"—an opportunity "to revamp all aspects of our societies and economies."[1] Even when the vision is not as grand, policy advice wrapped around the recovery from COVID-19 has advocated for significant changes. In its April 2021 *World Economic Outlook*, the IMF noted that policy priorities should involve overcoming the immediate crisis and limiting long-term economic scarring but should also include "bold action to limit emissions, particularly for the largest polluters" to respond to the threat of climate change.[2] On the other hand, there is a fear that the pandemic "will persist at dangerous levels for years to come" and that "the threat of future zoonotic or human-made pathogens will only rise over time" unless there is international cooperation to find the origins of the disease and take corrective action.[3] Aside from involving more control by governments, more coordination by multilateral agencies, and more attempts at influence from policy researchers, both of these

---

[1] World Economic Forum, "Now Is the Time for a 'Great Reset,'" June 3, 2020. In the United States, this coincided with a new social movement led by elite institutions to treat people differently based on race, ethnicity, and other immutable characteristics.

[2] IMF, 2021b, p. 16.

[3] Monica de Bolle, Maurice Obstfeld, and Adam S. Posen, "Economic Policy for a Pandemic Age: An Introduction," in Monica de Bolle, Maurice Obstfeld, and Adam S. Posen, eds., *Economic Policy for a Pandemic Age: How the World Must Prepare*, Washington, D.C.: Peterson Institute for International Economics, PIIE Briefing 21-2, April 2021, p. 4.

visions signal significant disruptions of and encourage large changes to the conduct of daily life.

Despite those visions, what is notable is how little the geoeconomic balance has changed, at least as of the end of August 2021. China and the United States are still the leading economies and have been the best-performing major economies during the pandemic. The United States' European and Japanese allies have further receded relative to the global economy. China and Russia have tried to increase their global influence through vaccine diplomacy, although results are mixed. The broad network of the United States with its allies and partners has the potential to widely distribute effective vaccines worldwide and show their strength but has so far fallen short.

But what is also notable is the uncertainty. Even China, which had been billed as successfully controlling the disease in 2020 and developed its own vaccines, faced new outbreaks in 2021.[4] Most of the uncertainty going forward, however, is likely to emanate from the regions left out of most discussions of global competition: Africa and Latin America, or more broadly, the developing world.

Beyond Growth and the Geoeconomic Balance

As of August 2021, the COVID-19 pandemic had numerous consequences beyond those discussed in this report, consequences that are likely to influence global and national economic performance. As with the effects described so far, however, these consequences are still uncertain.

Globalization

One notable area that the pandemic affected was globalization. Initially, world merchandise trade was projected to decline by 12.9 percent in 2020 in

---

[4] Talha Burki, "China's Successful Control of COVID-19," *The Lancet*, Vol. 20, No. 11, November 2020, pp. 1240–1241 (published online October 8, 2020, then updated and corrected October 22, 2020); Sha Hua, "China Escalates Efforts to Beat Back Its Worst Covid-19 Resurgence," *Wall Street Journal*, January 20, 2021; "China Re-Imposes Travel Curbs on Province After Virus Cases," Associated Press, May 30, 2021.

an optimistic scenario and 31.9 percent in a pessimistic scenario.[5] And, in fact, it fell by 6 percent in the first quarter of 2020 relative to the first quarter of 2019 and 21 percent in the second quarter of 2020 relative to the second quarter of 2019.[6] However, a trade rebound in June and July 2020 moved projections upward, with the full-year 2020 projection improving to a 9.2 percent decrease. The actual result was a 5.3 percent decrease, less dire than projected but still a sizable decrease.[7] Likewise, foreign direct investment experienced a large decrease, falling 42 percent from $1.5 trillion in 2019 to a preliminary estimate of $859 billion in 2020, the lowest level since 2004.[8]

With global merchandise trade projected to increase by 8 percent in 2021 and then 4 percent in 2022, it appears that trade will reach its prepandemic levels, although it will not immediately return to its prepandemic trend.[9] However, there has been significant variation by country and region. This can be found with foreign direct investment as well, in which inflows of investments into the economically advanced countries accounted for nearly the entire decline, and investments into developing economies, especially those of Asia, held steady. Furthermore, travel, which is important for services trade (despite the increasing use of video meetings), crashed during the pandemic. International tourist arrivals, for example, fell 73 percent in 2020 relative to 2019.[10] As of late summer 2021, global travel remained well below that of previous years, with numerous restrictions, including broad restrictions by the United States on travelers from Europe and the reinstitu-

---

[5] World Trade Organization, "Trade Falls Steeply in First Half of 2020," press release, Geneva, Switzerland, June 22, 2020a.

[6] World Trade Organization, "Trade Shows Signs of Rebound from COVID-19, Recovery Still Uncertain," press release, Geneva, Switzerland, October 6, 2020b.

[7] World Trade Organization, "World Trade Primed for Strong but Uneven Recovery After COVID-19 Pandemic Shock," press release, Geneva, Switzerland, March 31, 2021.

[8] United Nations Conference on Trade and Development, *Investment Trends Monitor*, Genva, Switzerland, Issue 38, January 2021; United Nations Conference on Trade and Development, "Foreign Direct Investment: Inward and Outward Flows and Stock, Annual," online database, data as of December 1, 2020.

[9] World Trade Organization, 2021.

[10] United Nations World Tourism Organization, "UNWTO Tourism Data Dashboard: International Tourism and COVID-19," online database, undated.

tion in August 2021 of the EU's removal of the United States from its list of countries that are safe for nonessential travel.[11]

The effects of these changes in global exchange are uncertain. With travel remaining under its previous levels, economies that depend on tourism are likely to continue to suffer, as was seen in the EU in 2020. Likewise, services trade could remain well below trend; because the advanced economies depend more heavily on services trade than do the developing economies, travel restrictions could slow the full recovery of the advanced economies. And as noted in preceding chapters, countries have considered localizing production in certain sectors as protection against future pandemic-related or other disruptions. Doing so would have short-term costs but could build in the ability to recover faster when the inevitable future disruptions occur.

National Cohesion

The pandemic is likely to have effects well beyond economic growth and even distribution and employment. Outside the economic realm, there might be an impact on national cohesion, sparked by widening inequality and high levels of unemployment or reduced incomes among sectors of the population in each country around the world. Other consequences from the way governments have handled the pandemic could include reduced support for government and reduced trust in expertise. Accordingly, an understanding of the full effects of the pandemic should include analysis of measures of national progress in human development, quality of governance, and democratization.

Policy Coordination

The pandemic occurred at a time of heightened nationalism and rivalry. During 2020, coordination among the G-7 advanced economies and between those advanced economies and China stumbled, but other forms of coordination succeeded. The international economic response to the pandemic, especially through the World Bank and IMF, mobilized both debt relief and

---

[11] Samuel Petrequin, "EU Takes US Off Safe Travel List; Backs Travel Restrictions," Associated Press, August 30, 2021.

new capital injections. In addition, central banks around the world took actions that not only benefited their own countries but the global economy. As in the global financial crisis of 2008 and 2009, parts of the global economic order kept functioning, this time when national governments were at loggerheads. Given that there are likely to be future global crises, a greater understanding of why coordination continued and how it can be enhanced, even when national governments are uncooperative, would be valuable.

Policy Implications for the United States

From an economic and social standpoint, COVID-19 upended the United States. But in some ways, the pandemic continued and at times accelerated global trends, such as the U.S.-China rivalry. The United States instituted various new measures in the economic realm, and China became both more assertive, such as in its crackdown on Hong Kong, and less cooperative, such as in its refusal to fully cooperate on any investigation of the origins of COVID-19. But as of late summer 2021, the pandemic had not broken pre-existing global trends, however much policy entrepreneurs wished it were otherwise. Furthermore, the pandemic introduced several policy innovations but also policy challenges.

Policy Innovations and Updates Wrought by the Pandemic

Two notable policy moves might herald future changes in the United States and the EU. Operation Warp Speed was an example of industrial policy that succeeded as it was meant to, accelerating the introduction of vaccines to market. Therefore, it might make policymakers across the political spectrum more open to greater government intervention in the economy, particularly in research and development and in innovation, where there are large, fixed costs and where there might be benefits to coordination. Alternatively, policymakers might view the effort as equivalent to a wartime measure where results are far more important than cost, and they might therefore be averse to similar programs during normal times. But a model has been established and could be adapted for the future, much as Operation Warp Speed was itself built on a two-decade foundation.[12] Across the Atlantic, the new, large EU bond issuance could introduce greater fiscal cooperation to the EU, potentially stabilize growth, and make the euro more acceptable as a reserve currency, perhaps gaining ground on the dollar and edging out the RMB in small amounts.

The pandemic also showed that the boundaries of global competition are wide, and this competition now includes promises to safeguard the world's health. Vaccine diplomacy became an ongoing activity; Russia and China especially tried to show that they would be reliable partners to countries without the ability to make or procure their own vaccines. Although U.S. and EU missteps gave Russia and China good material to work with, Russia and China's track record in actually fulfilling their promises regarding both vaccine delivery and vaccine efficacy left much to be desired. This gave the EU, the UK, and the United States especially an opportunity to catch up. For that reason, any final judgment about the outcome of vaccine diplomacy efforts would be premature until the pandemic's end becomes much more of a reality.

Defense and Security Changes Wrought by the Pandemic

From a defense and security standpoint, changes were much more modest than the mid-2020 economic disruption indicated they might be. China continued to grow economically and modernize its armed forces. Russia's economy declined, but not as much as the economy of many other countries. And most of Russia's security activities are close to home and are relatively low cost, so combined with the 2021 rise in oil prices, the pandemic should not have major effects on Russia's activities. Accordingly, at least as of late spring 2021, the pandemic had not brought about significant changes in the capacity or polices of major competitors of the United States.

However, lower levels of growth in Japan and especially Europe heighten the continuing issue of how much U.S. allies and partners truly can contribute to collective defense efforts. Defense budgets in NATO allies have

---

[12] Eric D. Hargan and Robert Kadlec, "It Took Years to Reach Vaccine Warp Speed," *Wall Street Journal*, September 24, 2021.

been rising relative to that of the United States. In 2014, only two non-U.S. NATO members had defense budgets of at least 2 percent of their GDP in real terms, the agreed-upon NATO percentage.[13] It was estimated that ten non-U.S. members would meet this mark by 2020. Likewise, although the non-U.S. share of NATO defense expenditures averaged 27.8 percent from 2013 through 2016, it averaged 30.5 percent from 2017 through 2020.[14]

This trend might be at risk because of economic underperformance among allies. In a small sign, NATO decreased its estimate of non-U.S. 2020 defense expenditures from $313 billion in an October 2020 estimate to $311 billion in a March 2021 estimate.[15] U.S. defense planners might need to consider contingencies in which the European contribution to a joint effort will be more limited than that provided for by current plans. U.S. allies might need to make difficult choices about reprioritizing defense expenditures. Given its ability to borrow and its relatively better economic performance, the United States will have more freedom to choose its defense expenditures but might decide to redirect federal spending for other purposes, such as health care, infrastructure, social programs, or—should interest rates rise—debt service.

As of late summer 2021, the risk of declining U.S. budgets had not manifested. President Biden's proposed fiscal year 2022 budget raises defense spending from $735 billion in 2021 to $754 billion in 2022, and increases are projected through at least 2031.[16] Furthermore, concern about the effects on the defense budget of rising U.S. debt and pressures to fund nondefense spending has been an ongoing issue, so again, at least in terms of the United States, the pandemic does not herald a major break.

Finally, the pandemic showed gaps in U.S. global leadership and alliance management. In 2020, the United States and its allies did not partner

---

[13] NATO, "Defence Expenditure of NATO Countries (2013–2020)," press release, Brussels, Communiqué PR/CP(2021)030, March 16, 2021. Values are in 2015 prices and exchange rates.

[14] This is based on 2020 *estimated* expenditures.

[15] NATO, "Defence Expenditure of NATO Countries (2013–2020)," press release, Brussels, Communiqué PR/CP(2020)104, October 21, 2020; NATO, 2021. Values are in 2015 prices and exchange rates.

[16] White House, Office of Management and Budget, 2021.

in vaccine development or distribution. As the actions by the G-7 and the Quad in early 2021 showed, this might have started to change, especially as the vaccination rates in the advanced economies continue to rise and these economies have more vaccine supply to share. But a slow response to India's emergency, charges of hoarding vaccine doses, and disagreements with allies over the issue of vaccine patents indicate that the United States will continue to face challenges balancing U.S. interests and global interests where these conflict.[17]

---

[17] Thomas Wright, "Biden's Misstep in India," *The Atlantic*, April 28, 2021; Adam Taylor and Emily Rauhala, "U.S. Could Have 300 Million Extra Vaccine Doses by End of July, Raising Concerns About Hoarding," *Washington Post*, April 15, 2021.

Abbreviations

COVAX	COVID-19 Vaccines Global Access
COVID-19	coronavirus disease 2019
EU	European Union
G-7	Group of Seven
GDP	gross domestic product
IMF	International Monetary Fund
NATO	North Atlantic Treaty Organization
PMI	purchasing managers' index
RMB	renminbi
UK	United Kingdom

References

Abraham, Roshan, and Kavya B., "Global COVID-19 Cases Surpass 200 Mln as Delta Variant Spreads," Reuters, August 4, 2021.

Aris, Ben, "Russian Government Launches a National Projects 2.0 Revamp," BNE Intellinews, February 5, 2021.

Aris, Ben, and Ivan Tkachev, "Long Read: 20 Years of Russia's Economy Under Putin, in Numbers," *Moscow Times*, August 19, 2019.

Australian Bureau of Statistics, "Australian National Accounts: National Income, Expenditure and Product; Quarterly Estimates of Key Economic Flows in Australia, Including Gross Domestic Product (GDP), Consumption, Investment, Income and Saving; Reference Period December 2020," March 3, 2021a. As of September 1, 2021:
https://www.abs.gov.au/statistics/economy/national-accounts/australian-national-accounts-national-income-expenditure-and-product/dec-2020

———, "Australian National Accounts: National Income, Expenditure and Product; Quarterly Estimates of Key Economic Flows in Australia, Including Gross Domestic Product (GDP), Consumption, Investment, Income and Saving; Reference Period June 2021," September 1, 2021b. As of September 1, 2021:
https://www.abs.gov.au/statistics/economy/national-accounts/australian-national-accounts-national-income-expenditure-and-product/latest-release

Baker, Stephanie, and Cynthia Koons, "Inside Operation Warp Speed's $18 Billion Sprint for a Vaccine," *Bloomberg*, October 29, 2020.

Bank of England, Monetary Policy Committee, "In Focus: Uncertainty and Brexit," in Bank of England, *Monetary Policy Report*, London, November 2019, pp. 38–43.

Bank of Russia, "International Reserves of the Russian Federation (End of Period)," database, last updated May 1, 2021a. As of May 25, 2021:
http://www.cbr.ru/eng/hd_base/mrrf/mrrf_m/?UniDbQuery.Posted=True&UniDbQuery.From=01%2F2020&UniDbQuery.To=05%2F2021

———, "The Bank of Russia Increases the Key Rate by 100 b.p., to 6.50% p.a.," press release, Moscow, July 23, 2021b.

Barchuk, Anton, Mikhail Cherkashin, Anna Bulina, Natalia Berezina, Tatyana Rakova, Darya Kuplevatskaya, Oksana Stanevich, Dmitriy Skougarevskiy, and Artemiy Okhotin, "Vaccine Effectiveness Against Referral to Hospital and Severe Lung Injury Associated with COVID-19: A Population-Based Case-Control Study in St. Petersburg, Russia," MedRxiv, Preprint Server for Health Sciences, August 25, 2021.

Barry, Colleen, and Daria Litvinova, "Russia to Make Sputnik V Vaccine in Italy, a First in EU," Associated Press, March 9, 2021.

Benoit, Bertrand, Giovanni Legorano, and Nick Kostov, "Europe's Troubled COVID-19 Vaccine Rollout Turns the Corner," *Wall Street Journal*, May 4, 2021.

Bernstein, Jared, and Ernie Tedeschi, "Pandemic Prices: Assessing Inflation in the Months and Years Ahead," *Council of Economic Advisers*, blog, White House, April 12, 2021. As of May 27, 2021:
https://www.whitehouse.gov/cea/blog/2021/04/12/
pandemic-prices-assessing-inflation-in-the-months-and-years-ahead/

Biswas, Soutik, "COVID-19: Has India's Deadly Second Wave Peaked?" BBC, May 26, 2021.

Blackwill, Robert D., and Thomas Wright, "Why COVID-19 Presents a World Reordering Moment," *National Interest*, July 11, 2020.

Board of Governors of the Federal Reserve System, "Federal Reserve Announces Extensive New Measures to Support the Economy," press release, Washington, D.C., March 23, 2020a.

———, "Credit and Liquidity Programs and Balance Sheet," last updated July 9, 2020b. As of May 28, 2021:
https://www.federalreserve.gov/monetarypolicy/bst_fedsbalancesheet.htm

———, "China / U.S. Foreign Exchange Rate [DEXCHUS]," FRED, Federal Reserve Bank of St. Louis, last updated May 24, 2021a. As of May 27, 2021:
https://fred.stlouisfed.org/series/DEXCHUS

———, "Factors Affecting Reserve Balances," statistical release, H.4.1, May 27, 2021b. As of May 28, 2021:
https://www.federalreserve.gov/releases/h41/current/h41.htm

———, "Factors Affecting Reserve Balances," statistical release data download program, H.4.1, May 27, 2021c. As of May 28, 2021:
https://www.federalreserve.gov/datadownload/Choose.aspx?rel=H41

———, Z.1. *Financial Accounts of the United States: Flow of Funds, Balance Sheets, and Integrated Macroeconomic Accounts, First Quarter 2021, Federal Reserve Statistical Release,* Washington, D.C., June 20, 2021d.

————, "Distribution of Household Wealth in the U.S. Since 1989," DFA: Distributional Financial Accounts, online database, last updated June 21, 2021e. As of August 16, 2021:
https://www.federalreserve.gov/releases/z1/dataviz/dfa/distribute/chart/

de Bolle, Monica, Maurice Obstfeld, and Adam S. Posen, "Economic Policy for a Pandemic Age: An Introduction," in Monica de Bolle, Maurice Obstfeld, and Adam S. Posen, eds., *Economic Policy for a Pandemic Age: How the World Must Prepare*, Washington, D.C.: Peterson Institute for International Economics, PIIE Briefing 21-2, April 2021, pp. 3–9.

Bridge, "China COVID-19 Vaccine Tracker," last updated August 30, 2021. As of August 30, 2021:
https://bridgebeijing.com/our-publications/our-publications-1/china-covid-19-vaccines-tracker/

Bucci, Enrico M., Johannes Berkhof, André Gillibert, Gowri Gopalakrishna, Raffaele A. Calogero, and Lex M. Bouter, "Data Discrepancies and Substandard Reporting of Interim Data of Sputnik V Phase 3 Trial," *The Lancet*, Vol. 397, No. 10288, May 22, 2021, pp. 1881–1883.

Burki, Talha, "China's Successful Control of COVID-19," *The Lancet*, Vol. 20, No. 11, November 2020, pp. 1240–1241.

Campbell, Kurt M., and Rush Doshi, "The Coronavirus Could Reshape Global Order," *Foreign Affairs*, March 18, 2020.

Cheng, Jonathan, "China Growth Numbers Betray Waning Momentum," *Wall Street Journal*, April 16, 2021a.

————, "Chinese Economy Grew More than 18% in First Quarter," *Wall Street Journal*, April 16, 2021b.

"China Re-Imposes Travel Curbs on Province After Virus Cases," Associated Press, May 30, 2021.

"China Rejects WHO Call for Renewed Probe into Origins of COVID-19," *France 24*, August 13, 2021.

"China Removes All Remaining Counties from Poverty List," Xinhua, November 23, 2020.

"Chinese Ports Choke over China's 'Zero Tolerance' COVID-19 Policy," Reuters, August 17, 2021.

Cordell, Jake, "State-Run Bank Says Russia Unlikely to Meet Economic Targets 'Without More Active Policies,'" *Moscow Times*, November 20, 2019.

"Coronavirus: Northern Italy Quarantines 16 Million People," BBC, March 8, 2020.

"Covid: China's Sinovac Vaccine Gets WHO Emergency Approval," BBC, June 2, 2021.

"COVID Vaccines: Without WHO Approval, Covaxin Remains Second Among Equals," The Wire, May 25, 2021.

Crossley, Gabriel, "China Rejects WHO Plan for Study of COVID-19 Origin," Reuters, July 22, 2021.

Cushing, Jonathan, "Is the Sputnik V Vaccine Too Good to Be True? Without the Data, It's Hard to Know," Stat, May 26, 2021.

Debre, Isabel, "UAE to Offer Booster Shot to Recipients of Sinopharm Vaccine," Associated Press, May 18, 2021.

Deutsch, Jillian, and Ashleigh Furlong, "EU Falls Behind China, US on Vaccine Donations: Document," *Politico*, August 2, 2021.

Dixon, Robyn, "Vaccine-Skippers Face Work Penalties," *Washington Post*, July 29, 2021.

Dobrovidova, Olga, "Russia's Sputnik V Protects Against Severe COVID-19 from Delta Variant, Study Shows," *Science*, August 26, 2021.

Dou, Eva, and Shibani Mahtani, "China's Vaccine Diplomacy Stumbles as Clinical Trial Data Remains Absent," *Washington Post*, March 23, 2021.

Dube, Ryan, "First Dose of Chinese Covid-19 Vaccine Offers Little Protection, Chile Learns," *Wall Street Journal*, April 18, 2021.

Economic and Social Research Office, Cabinet Office, Government of Japan, "Quarterly Estimates of GDP: January–March 2021 (1st Preliminary)," May 18, 2021a. As of May 30, 2021:
https://www.esri.cao.go.jp/en/sna/data/sokuhou/files/2021/qe211/gdemenuea.html

———, "Quarterly Estimates of GDP: April–June 2021 (1st Preliminary)," August 16, 2021b. As of September 1, 2021:
https://www.esri.cao.go.jp/en/sna/data/sokuhou/files/2021/qe212/gdemenuea.html

Ellis, R. Evan, "A Race Against Time: Deploying Vaccines and Addressing the Disproportionate Impacts of Covid-19 in Latin America and the Caribbean," testimony presented before the U.S. House of Representatives Subcommittee on the Western Hemisphere, Civilian Security, Migration, and International Economic Policy, Washington, D.C., May 13, 2021.

Emont, Jon, "Covid-19 Deaths Rise Sharply in Indonesia," *Wall Street Journal*, July 27, 2021.

Emont, Jon, and Lam Le, "Delta Variant Outbreaks in Sparsely Vaccinated Asian Countries Disrupt Production," *Wall Street Journal*, August 25, 2021.

Engzell, Per, Arun Frey, and Mark D. Verhagen, "Learning Loss Due to School Closures During the COVID-19 Pandemic," *PNAS*, Vol. 118, No. 17, 2021.

European Commission, "Recovery Plan for Europe," webpage, undated. As of June 1, 2021:
https://ec.europa.eu/info/strategy/recovery-plan-europe_en

———, "Europe's Moment: Repair and Prepare for the Next Generation," press release, Brussels, May 27, 2020.

———, "Vaccinating the World: 'Team Europe' to Share More than 200 Million Doses of COVID-19 Vaccines with Low and Middle-Income Countries by the End of 2021," press release, Brussels, July 22, 2021.

European Council, General Secretariat of the Council, "Special Meeting of the European Council (24 and 25 May 2021)—Conclusions," note to delegations, Brussels, May 25, 2021. As of May 28, 2021:
https://www.consilium.europa.eu/en/press/press-releases/2021/05/25/european-council-conclusions-24-25-may-2021/

European Union Chamber of Commerce in China, "COVID-19 Travel Control in Nanjing," Voice of European Business in China, email update, July 29, 2021.

Eurostat, "GDP and Main Components (Output, Expenditure and Income) [NAMA_10_GDP$DEFAULTVIEW]," spreadsheet from online database, last updated April 1, 2021a.

———, "GDP and Main Components (Output, Expenditure and Income) [NAMQ_10_GDP$DEFAULTVIEW]," spreadsheet from online database, last updated April 1, 2021b.

———, "Employment and Activity by Sex and Age—Quarterly Data [LFSI_EMP_Q__custom_1010160] (Seasonally Adjusted Data Not Calendar Adjusted Data)," spreadsheet from online database, last updated April 13, 2021c. As of May 30, 2021:
https://ec.europa.eu/eurostat/databrowser/view/LFSI_EMP_Q__custom_1010160/default/table

———, "GDP Down by 0.6% and Employment Down by 0.3% in the Euro Area; in the EU, GDP Down by 0.4% and Employment Down by 0.3%," GDP and Employment Flash Estimates for the First Quarter of 2021, 58/2021, May 18, 2021d.

———, "GDP Up by 2.0% and Employment Up by 0.5% in the Euro Area," GDP and Employment Flash Estimates for the Second Quarter of 2021, 94/2021, August 17, 2021e.

Fairless, Tom, and Paul Hannon, "Europe's Economic Recipe for the Pandemic: Keep Workers in Their Jobs," Wall Street Journal, March 24, 2020.

Farzan, Antonia Noori, and Claire Parker, "How Did the COVID-19 Outbreak in India Get So Bad?" Washington Post, April 28, 2021.

Faucon, Benoit, Georgi Kantchev, and Summer Said, "Russia Takes Aim at U.S. Shale Oil Producers," Wall Street Journal, March 13, 2020.

Federal Reserve Bank of New York, "Statement Regarding Treasury Reserve Management Purchases and Repurchase Operations," March 12, 2020.

Federal State Statistical Service (Rosstat), "Gross Domestic Product (at 2016 Prices, Bln Rubles)" ["Валовой внутрений продукт (в ценах 2016г., млрд. руб.)"], Tab 6b, spreadsheet, last updated April 1, 2021a.

———, "Production and Use of Gross Domestic Product (GDP) for 2020" ["О производстве и использовании валового внутреннего продукта (ВВП) за 2020 год"], April 1, 2021b.

———, "Rosstat Presents the Second GDP Estimate for 2020" ["Росстат представил вторую оценку ВВП за 2020 год"], News of Rosstat, April 1, 2021c.

———, "Rosstat Presents a Preliminary Estimate of GDP for the 1st Quarter of 2021" ["Росстат представляет предварительную оценку ВВП за I квартал 2021 года"], News of Rosstat, May 17, 2021d. As of May 25, 2021: https://rosstat.gov.ru/folder/313/document/122604

———, "On the Production of Gross Domestic Product (GDP) in the First Quarter of 2021" ["О производстве валового внутреннего продукта (ВВП) в I квартале 2021 года"], News of Rosstat, June 15, 2021e. As of August 30, 2021: https://gks.ru/bgd/free/B04_03/IssWWW.exe/Stg/d02/106.htm

———, "On a Preliminary Estimate of the Dynamics of GDP in the Second Quarter of 2021" ["О предварительной оценке динамики ВВП во II квартале 2021 года"], News of Rosstat, August 13, 2021f. As of August 30, 2021: https://gks.ru/bgd/free/B04_03/IssWWW.exe/Stg/d02/vvp1308.htm

Focus Economics, "Russia: Pace of Economic Contraction Softens in Q1," May 17, 2021.

Food and Agricultural Organization of the United Nations, "Hunger and Food Insecurity," webpage, undated. As of September 2, 2021: https://www.fao.org/hunger/en/

Garcia-Herrero, Alicia, "China's Debt Surge Moderated in Q4 2020 but Scars in Terms of Long-Term Growth Impact to Remain," LinkedIn Pulse, February 5, 2021a. As of May 24, 2021: https://www.linkedin.com/pulse/chinas-debt-surge-moderated-q4-2020-scars-terms-alicia-garcia-herrero/

———, "China's Strong Growth in Q1 Helped Debt Dynamics but for How Long?" LinkedIn Pulse, April 30, 2021b. As of May 24, 2021: https://www.linkedin.com/pulse/chinas-strong-growth-q1-helped-debt-dynamics-how-long-garcia-herrero/

Gavi, the Vaccine Alliance, "Donor Profiles," webpage, last updated March 31, 2021a. As of May 28, 2021:
https://www.gavi.org/investing-gavi/funding/donor-profiles

———, "COVAX Vaccine Roll-Out: Country Updates," webpage, last updated August 31, 2021b. As of August 31, 2021:
https://www.gavi.org/covax-vaccine-roll-out

Gill, Indermit, "Deep-Sixing Poverty in China," *Future Development*, blog, Brookings Institution, January 25, 2021. As of March 8, 2021:
https://www.brookings.edu/blog/future-development/2021/01/25/deep-sixing-poverty-in-china/

Government of the United Kingdom, "UK Begins Donating Millions of COVID-19 Vaccines Overseas," press release, London, July 28, 2021.

Gullo, Theresa, "Estimating the Federal Budgetary Effects of Pandemic-Related Legislation: A Presentation to the Association for Budgeting and Financial Management's 2020 Virtual Symposium," slide deck, Congressional Budget Office, September 25, 2020. As of May 27, 2020:
https://www.cbo.gov/system/files/2020-09/56633-ABFM-Presentation.pdf

Hafner, Marco, Erez Yerushalmi, Clement Fays, Elaine Dufresne, and Christian van Stolk, *COVID-19 and the Cost of Vaccine Nationalism*, Santa Monica, Calif., and Cambridge, UK: RAND Corporation, RR-A769-1, 2020. As of September 2, 2021:
https://www.rand.org/pubs/research_reports/RRA769-1.html

Hannon, Paul, Gabriele Steinhauser, and Sha Hua, "Delta Variant's Spread Hobbles Global Efforts to Lift Covid-19 Restrictions," *Wall Street Journal*, July 1, 2021.

Hargan, Eric D., and Robert Kadlec, "It Took Years to Reach Vaccine Warp Speed," *Wall Street Journal*, September 24, 2021.

Haseltine, William A., "What Can We Learn from Australia's COVID-19 Response?" *Forbes*, March 24, 2021.

Holder, Josh, "Tracking Coronavirus Vaccinations Around the World," *New York Times*, last updated September 3, 2021. As of September 3, 2021:
https://www.nytimes.com/interactive/2021/world/covid-vaccinations-tracker.html

Hua, Sha, "China Escalates Efforts to Beat Back Its Worst Covid-19 Resurgence," *Wall Street Journal*, January 20, 2021.

IMF—*See* International Monetary Fund.

International Energy Agency, *Global Energy Review 2021*, Paris, April 2021.

International Monetary Fund, *World Economic Outlook Update: An Update of the Key WEO Projections*, Washington, D.C., January 20, 2020a.

———, *World Economic Outlook Update: A Crisis Like No Other, an Uncertain Recovery*, Washington, D.C., June 2020b.

———, *Regional Economic Outlook Update: Europe*, Washington, D.C., April 2021a.

———, *World Economic Outlook: Managing Divergent Recoveries*, Washington, D.C., April 2021b.

———, "Russian Federation," Policy Responses to COVID-19: Policy Tracker, webpage, last updated May 7, 2021c. As of May 25, 2021: https://www.imf.org/en/Topics/imf-and-covid19/ Policy-Responses-to-COVID-19

———, *World Economic Outlook Update: Fault Lines Widen in the Global Recovery*, Washington, D.C., July 2021d.

———, "IMF Managing Director Announces the US$650 Billion SDR Allocation Comes into Effect," press release, Washington, D.C., August 23, 2021e.

Janicek, Karel, "Russia Wants Slovakia to Return Its Sputnik V Vaccines," Associated Press, April 8, 2021.

Jones, Ian, and Polly Roy, "Sputnik V COVID-19 Vaccine Candidate Appears Safe and Effective," *The Lancet*, Vol. 397, No. 10275, February 20, 2021, pp. 642–643.

Kahl, Colin, and Thomas Wright, *Aftershocks: Pandemic Politics and the End of the Old International Order*, New York: St. Martin's Press, 2021.

Kantchev, Georgi, "Russia's COVID-19 Vaccine Is Embraced Abroad, Snubbed at Home," *Wall Street Journal*, March 8, 2021.

Kaplan, Robert S., Tyler Atkinson, Jim Dolmas, Marc P. Giannoni, and Karel Mertens, "The Labor Market May Be Tighter than the Level of Employment Suggests," Federal Reserve Bank of Dallas, May 27, 2021. As of May 27, 2021: https://www.dallasfed.org/research/economics/2021/0527

Kingson, Jennifer A., "Exclusive: $1 Billion-Plus Riot Damage Is Most Expensive in Insurance History," *Axios*, September 16, 2020.

Korsunskaya, Darya, "Update 1—Russia's Economy Ministry Proposes Extra State Spending to Offset Rate Hikes," Reuters, August 5, 2021.

Krauss, Clifford, "Oil Nations, Prodded by Trump, Reach Deal to Slash Production," *New York Times*, April 12, 2020.

Kumar, Krishna, "Why America Must Do More to Vaccinate the World's Population," *National Interest*, May 3, 2021a.

———, "Vaccine Patents Debate Risks Becoming a Sideshow in the Global Battle Against COVID-19," *The Hill*, May 16, 2021b.

———, "Split-Screen Recovery from Pandemic Isn't Sustainable," *UPI*, July 20, 2021c.

Light, Felix, "Will Russia's Belated Promotion of Sputnik V at Home Sway a Doubting Public?" *Moscow Times*, April 7, 2021.

Mahler, Daniel Gerszon, Nishant Yonzan, Christoph Lakner, R. Andres Castaneda Aguilar, and Haoyu Wu, "Updated Estimates of the Impact of COVID-19 on Global Poverty: Turning the Corner on the Pandemic in 2021?" *Data Blog*, World Bank, June 24, 2021. As of September 2, 2021: https://blogs.worldbank.org/opendata/ updated-estimates-impact-covid-19-global-poverty-turning-corner-pandemic-2021

Malpass, David, "How to Vaccinate Every Country," *Voices: Perspectives on Development*, blog, World Bank, May 27, 2021. As of June 1, 2021: https://blogs.worldbank.org/voices/how-vaccinate-every-country

Mandhana, Niharika, "Asia Suffers Outbreaks Where COVID-19 Had Seemed Beaten," *Wall Street Journal*, May 19, 2021.

Mao, Frances, "'Fortress Australia': Why Calls to Open Up Borders Are Meeting Resistance," BBC, May 26, 2021.

Mardasov, Anton, "Kremlin's Vaccine Diplomacy Finds Trouble in Middle East," *Al-Monitor*, July 16, 2021.

McDonald, Joe, and Huizhong Wu, "Delta Variant Challenges China's Costly Lockdown Strategy," Associated Press, August 5, 2021.

Miller, Hugo, and Ania Nussbaum, "Merkel, Macron Back $8 Billion Virus Vaccine Fund Effort," *Bloomberg*, April 24, 2020.

Miller, Michael E., "Australia, Once a Pandemic Hero, Now Struggles with Vaccination," *Washington Post*, July 18, 2021.

Ministry of External Affairs, Government of India, "Vaccine Supply: Made-in-India COVID-19 Vaccine Supplies So Far (in Lakhs)," COVID-19 Updates, webpage, last updated May 29, 2021. As of September 3, 2021: https://www.mea.gov.in/vaccine-supply.htm

Ministry of Finance of the Russian Federation, "Annual Report on Execution of the Federal Budget (Starting from January 1, 2006)," Federal Budget of the Russian Federation, webpage, last updated April 15, 2021a. As of May 26, 2021: https://minfin.gov.ru/en/statistics/fedbud/ ?id_65=119255-annual_report_on_execution_of_the_federal_budget_starting_from_january_1_2006

———, "Volume of the National Wealth Fund," Statistics, webpage, last updated August 9, 2021b. As of August 9, 2021: https://minfin.gov.ru/en/key/nationalwealthfund/ statistics/?id_65=104686-volume_of_the_national_wealth_fund

Ministry of Statistics and Programme Implementation, Government of India, "Annual and Quarterly Estimates of GDP at Constant Prices (2011-12 Series)," Excel spreadsheet, March 5, 2021a. As of May 30, 2021: http://mospi.nic.in/data

————, "Annual and Quarterly Estimates of GDP at Constant Prices (2011–12 Series)," Excel spreadsheet, June 1, 2021b. As of September 1, 2021: http://mospi.nic.in/data

Morrow, James, "Covid Mania Returns Australia to Its Roots as a Nation of Prisoners," *Wall Street Journal*, July 25, 2021.

Moutinho, Sofia, and Meredith Wadman, "Is Russia's COVID-19 Vaccine Safe? Brazil's Veto of Sputnik V Sparks Lawsuit Threat and Confusion," *Science*, April 30, 2021.

Mouton, Christopher A., Russell Hanson, Adam R. Grissom, and John P. Godges, *COVID-19 Air Traffic Visualization: COVID-19 Cases in China Were Likely 37 Times Higher than Reported in January 2020*, Santa Monica, Calif.: RAND Corporation, RR-A248-3, 2020. As of April 26, 2021: https://www.rand.org/pubs/research_reports/RRA248-3.html

National Bureau of Statistics of China, "Gross Domestic Product? Growth Rate (Preceding Quarter = 100)(%)," webpage, undated. As of May 24, 2021: https://data.stats.gov.cn/english/easyquery.htm?cn=B01

————, "Announcement of the National Bureau of Statistics on the Final Verification of GDP in 2019," press release, Beijing, December 30, 2020.

————, "Preliminary Accounting Results of GDP for the Fourth Quarter and the Whole Year of 2020," press release, Beijing, January 20, 2021a.

————, "Statistical Communiqué of the People's Republic of China on the 2020 National Economic and Social Development," press release, Beijing, February 28, 2021b.

————, "National Economy Made a Good Start in the First Quarter," press release, Beijing, April 16, 2021c.

————, "Preliminary Accounting Results of GDP for the Second Quarter and the First Half Year of 2021," webpage, July 19, 2021d. As of July 23, 2021: http://www.stats.gov.cn/english/PressRelease/202107/t20210719_1819688.html

————, "Purchasing Managers Index for August 2021," webpage, September 1, 2021e. As of September 1, 2021: http://www.stats.gov.cn/english/PressRelease/202109/t20210901_1821512.html

National Health Commission of the People's Republic of China, "Over 700 Mln COVID-19 Vaccine Doses Administered Across China," Xinhua, June 4, 2021a.

———, "Over 2.05 Bln Doses of COVID-19 Vaccines Administered in China," *Xinhua*, September 1, 2021b.

NATO—*See* North Atlantic Treaty Organization.

Noack, Rick, "Vaccine-Skeptic France, Germany Inch Toward Near-Mandates," *Washington Post*, July 18, 2021.

North Atlantic Treaty Organization, "Defence Expenditure of NATO Countries (2013–2020)," press release, Brussels, Communiqué PR/CP(2020)104, October 21, 2020.

———, "Defence Expenditure of NATO Countries (2013–2020)," press release, Brussels, Communiqué PR/CP(2021)030, March 16, 2021.

Office for National Statistics (United Kingdom), "GDP Quarterly National Accounts, UK: October to December 2020," statistical bulletin, March 31, 2021a. As of April 2, 2021:
https://www.ons.gov.uk/economy/grossdomesticproductgdp/bulletins/quarterlynationalaccounts/octobertodecember2020

———, "GDP First Quarterly Estimate, UK: January to March 2021," statistical bulletin, May 12, 2021b. As of May 30, 2021:
https://www.ons.gov.uk/economy/grossdomesticproductgdp/bulletins/gdpfirstquarterlyestimateuk/januarytomarch2021

———, "GDP First Quarterly Estimate, UK: April to June 2021," statistical bulletin, August 12, 2021c. As of September 1, 2021:
https://www.ons.gov.uk/economy/grossdomesticproductgdp/bulletins/gdpfirstquarterlyestimateuk/apriltojune2021

Office of the U.S. Trade Representative, "Statement from Ambassador Katherine Tai on the COVID-19 Trips Waiver," Washington, D.C., May 5, 2021.

Onye Nkuzi [@cchukudebelu], "There's a 'great power competition to finance infrastructure in Africa' in the tweets of Western geopolitical analysts," Twitter post, March 7, 2021. As of June 9, 2021:
https://twitter.com/cchukudebelu/status/1368656025855918086

Organisation for Economic Co-operation and Development, *Perspectives on Global Development 2021: From Protest to Progress?* Paris: OECD Publishing, 2021.

Orlova, Natalia, "Russian National Projects During the Crisis Period," *Expert Opinions*, Valdai Discussion Club blog, May 1, 2020. As of May 26, 2021:
https://valdaiclub.com/a/highlights/russian-national-projects-during-the-crisis-period/

Ostroukh, Andrey, "Russia's Economic Recovery Faces COVID-19, Inflation Headwinds," Reuters, July 5, 2021.

Our World in Data, "COVID-19 Data Explorer," webpage, undated. As of September 1, 2021:
https://ourworldindata.org/explorers/coronavirus-data-explorer

Peel, Michael, David Pilling, and Stephanie Findlay, "Covax Scrambles to Make Up Vaccine Shortfall Due to Indian Export Halt," *Financial Times*, May 21, 2021.

Petrequin, Samuel, "EU Takes US Off Safe Travel List; Backs Travel Restrictions," Associated Press, August 30, 2021.

Plender, John, "The Demise of the Dollar? Reserve Currencies in the Era of 'Going Big,'" *Financial Times*, May 25, 2021.

Putin, Vladimir, "Message from the President to the Federal Assembly," Moscow, April 21, 2021. As of April 21, 2021:
http://kremlin.ru/events/president/news/65418

"Putin's 'Great Society' Program: Russian Government Outlines 12 Major National Projects," TASS, February 11, 2019.

Quinn, Colm, "U.S. Announces Plans to Export Its AstraZeneca Vaccine Stockpile," *Foreign Policy*, April 27, 2021.

Rees, Jon, and Rehan Ahmad, "EU Will Be Big New Player in Bond Market with Likely Triple-A Asset," S&P Global, August 3, 2020.

Ries, Charles P., Marco Hafner, Clement Fays, and Erez Yerushalmi, *The End of the Beginning: Assessing the Potential Economic Implications of Prolonged UK-EU Trade Policy Uncertainty*, Santa Monica, Calif.: RAND Corporation, RR-4265-RC, 2020. As of July 29, 2021:
https://www.rand.org/pubs/research_reports/RR4265.html

Romm, Tony, and Seung Min Kim, "Senate Republicans Make New Infrastructure Offer as House Democrats Urge Biden to Dig In," *Washington Post*, May 27, 2021.

Roy, Rajesh, and Vibhuti Agarwal, "India Suspends COVID-19 Vaccine Exports to Focus on Domestic Immunization," *Wall Street Journal*, March 25, 2021.

"Russia Resets Ambitious National Development Plan," *Moscow Times*, July 13, 2020.

Russian Direct Investment Fund, "Single Dose Vaccine, Sputnik Light, Authorized for Use in Russia," press release, Moscow, May 6, 2021a.

———, "RDIF and Panacea Biotec Launch the Production of Sputnik V in India," press release, Moscow, May 24, 2021b.

———, "RDIF and UNICEF Sign Sputnik V Vaccine Supply Agreement," press release, Moscow, May 27, 2021c.

———, "Indonesia Becomes the 70th Country to Approve the Sputnik V Vaccine," press release, Moscow, August 25, 2021d.

Schmidt, Fabian, "Coronavirus: How Effective Are the Chinese Vaccines?" DW, February 1, 2021.

Shatz, Howard J., "The Long-Term Budget Shortfall and National Security: A Problem the United States Should Stop Avoiding," *War on the Rocks*, November 6, 2017.

———, "COVID-19 and Economic Competition with China and Russia," *War on the Rocks*, August 31, 2020.

Shatz, Howard J., and Nathan Chandler, *Global Economic Trends and the Future of Warfare: The Changing Global Environment and Its Implications for the U.S. Air Force*, Santa Monica, Calif.: RAND Corporation, RR-2849/4-AF, 2020. As of April 26, 2021:
https://www.rand.org/pubs/research_reports/RR2849z4.html

Shepherd, Christian, and Primrose Riordan, "China Lacks Covid Exit Strategy as It Strives for Zero Infections," *Financial Times*, July 20, 2021.

Shulkin, David, "What Health Care Can Learn from Operation Warp Speed," commentary, *NEJM Catalyst*, January 21, 2021. As of June 7, 2021:
https://catalyst.nejm.org/doi/full/10.1056/CAT.21.0001

Shurkin, Michael, Alexander Noyes, and Mary Kate Adgie, *The COVID-19 Pandemic in Sub-Saharan Africa: An Opportunity to Rethink Strategic Competition on the Continent*, Santa Monica, Calif.: RAND Corporation, PE-A1055-1, 2021. As of September 2, 2021:
https://www.rand.org/pubs/perspectives/PEA1055-1.html

"Sinopharm: Chinese Covid Vaccine Gets WHO Emergency Approval," BBC, May 7, 2021.

Slaoui, Moncef, and Matthew Hepburn, "Perspective: Developing Safe and Effective Covid Vaccines—Operation Warp Speed's Strategy and Approach," *New England Journal of Medicine*, Vol. 383, No. 18, October 29, 2020, pp. 1701–1703.

"Slovakia Becomes 2nd EU Country to Approve Russia's Sputnik," Associated Press, May 26, 2021.

Smyth, Jamie, "How Australia Brought the Coronavirus Pandemic Under Control," *Financial Times*, November 13, 2020.

Statistics Canada, "Gross Domestic Product, Income and Expenditure, Fourth Quarter 2020," *The Daily*, March 2, 2021a.

———, "Table 36-10-0104-01 Gross Domestic Product, Expenditure-Based, Canada, Quarterly (x 1,000,000)," downloaded April 2, 2021b. As of April 2, 2021:
https://www150.statcan.gc.ca/t1/tbl1/en/tv.action?pid=3610010401

Steinhauser, Gabriele, Drew Hinshaw, and Betsy McKay, "Why a Grand Plan to Vaccinate the World Against COVID Unraveled," *Wall Street Journal*, May 26, 2021.

Steinhauser, Gabriele, and Joe Parkinson, "Third Covid Wave Upends Fragile South Africa, a Warning for the Developing World," *Wall Street Journal*, July 19, 2021.

Su, Alice, "China Fulfills a Dream to End Poverty. Not All Poor People Are Feeling Better Off," *Los Angeles Times*, November 27, 2020.

Subran, Ludovic, Alexis Garatti, Françoise Huang, and Georges Dib, "The Irony of Biden's Super Stimulus: USD360Bn for Exporters Around the World," Allianz Research, March 15, 2021.

Summers, Lawrence H., "The Inflation Risk Is Real," *Washington Post*, May 24, 2021.

Surie, Mandakini D., "India's Vaccine Diplomacy: Made in India, Shared with the World," *DevPolicy Blog*, March 29, 2021. As of May 30, 2021:
https://devpolicy.org/
indias-vaccine-diplomacy-made-in-india-shared-with-the-world-20210329/

Swagel, Phillip L., Director, U.S. Congressional Budget Office, "Preliminary Estimate of the Effects of H.R. 748, the CARES Act, Public Law 116-136, Revised, with Corrections to the Revenue Effect of the Employee Retention Credit and to the Modification of a Limitation on Losses for Taxpayers Other Than Corporations," analysis to Honorable Mike Enzi, Chairman, Committee on the Budget, U.S. Senate, revised April 27, 2020. As of May 27, 2021:
https://www.cbo.gov/publication/56334

Taylor, Adam, and Emily Rauhala, "U.S. Could Have 300 Million Extra Vaccine Doses by End of July, Raising Concerns About Hoarding," *Washington Post*, April 15, 2021.

Tett, Gillian, "When Economic Tribes Go to War," *Financial Times*, May 20, 2021.

Twining, Daniel, and Patrick Quirk, "Winning the Great Power Competition Post-Pandemic," *American Interest*, May 11, 2020.

United Nations, Department of Economic and Social Affairs, Population Division, "World Population Prospects 2019," online database, 2019. As of May 26, 2021:
https://population.un.org/wpp/DataQuery/

United Nations Conference on Trade and Development, "Foreign Direct Investment: Inward and Outward Flows and Stock, Annual," online database, data as of December 1, 2020. As of September 5, 2021: https://unctadstat.unctad.org/wds/TableViewer/ tableView.aspx?ReportId=96740

———, *Investment Trends Monitor*, Geneva, Switzerland, Issue 38, January 2021.

United Nations World Tourism Organization, "UNWTO Tourism Data Dashboard: International Tourism and COVID-19," online database, undated. As of September 5, 2021: https://www.unwto.org/international-tourism-and-covid-19

U.S. Bureau of Economic Analysis, "Current-Dollar and 'Real' Gross Domestic Product," Excel spreadsheet gdplev.xlsx, March 25, 2021a. As of March 29, 2021: https://apps.bea.gov/national/xls/gdplev.xlsx

———, "Gross Domestic Product (Third Estimate), GDP by Industry, and Corporate Profits, Fourth Quarter and Year 2020," news release, Suitland, Md., BEA 21–11, March 25, 2021b.

———, "Gross Domestic Product, First Quarter 2021 (Advance Estimate)," news release, Suitland, Md., BEA 21–18, April 29, 2021c.

———, "Personal Income and Outlays, March 2021," BEA 21–19, April 30, 2021d. As of May 27, 2021: https://www.bea.gov/news/2021/personal-income-and-outlays-march-2021

———, "Current-Dollar and 'Real' Gross Domestic Product," Excel spreadsheet gdplev.xlsx, July 29, 2021e.

———, "Gross Domestic Product, Second Quarter 2021 (Advance Estimate) and Annual Update," BEA 21–36, July 29, 2021f. As of August 16, 2021: https://www.bea.gov/news/2021/gross-domestic-product-second-quarter-2021-advance-estimate-and-annual-update

———, "Personal Income and Outlays, July 2021," BEA 21–41, August 27, 2021g. As of September 6, 2021: https://www.bea.gov/data/income-saving/personal-income

———, "Table 2.1. Personal Income and Its Disposition," *National Income and Product Accounts*, interactive data, last updated August 27, 2021h. As of August 27, 2021: https://apps.bea.gov/iTable/index_nipa.cfm

U.S. Bureau of Labor Statistics, "All Employees, Thousands, Total Nonfarm, Seasonally Adjusted," Series ID CES0000000001, Employment, Hours, and Earnings from the Current Employment Statistics Survey (National), online data, extracted May 25, 2021, and September 5, 2021. As of September 5, 2021:
https://beta.bls.gov/dataQuery/find?fq=survey:%5bce%5d&q=ce

U.S. Congressional Budget Office, "CBO Estimate for H.R. 266, the Paycheck Protection Program and Health Care Enhancement Act as Passed by the Senate on April 21, 2020," April 22, 2020. As of May 27, 2021:
https://www.cbo.gov/publication/56338

———, "Summary Estimate for Divisions M Through FF, H.R. 133, Consolidated Appropriations Act, 2021, Public Law 116-260, Enacted on December 27, 2020," January 14, 2021a. As of May 27, 2021:
https://www.cbo.gov/publication/56963

———, *The Budget and Economic Outlook: 2021 to 2031*, Washington, D.C., February 11, 2021b.

———, *The 2021 Long-Term Budget Outlook*, Washington, D.C., March 4, 2021c.

———, "Estimated Budgetary Effects of H.R. 1319, American Rescue Plan Act of 2021, as Passed by the Senate on March 6, 2021," cost estimate, March 10, 2021d. As of May 27, 2021:
https://www.cbo.gov/publication/57056

U.S. Department of State, "Secretary Antony J. Blinken Remarks to the Press on the COVID Response," briefing, April 5, 2021a.

———, "COVID-19 Vaccine Donations," webpage, data last updated August 27, 2021b. As of September 3, 2021:
https://www.state.gov/covid-19-recovery/vaccine-deliveries/

U.S. Department of the Treasury, "Debt to the Penny," online database, undated a. As of May 28, 2021:
https://fiscaldata.treasury.gov/datasets/debt-to-the-penny/debt-to-the-penny

———, "Securities (B): Portfolio Holdings of U.S. and Foreign Securities," Treasury International Capital System, undated b. As of May 28, 2021:
https://home.treasury.gov/data/
treasury-international-capital-tic-system-home-page/tic-forms-instructions/
securities-b-portfolio-holdings-of-us-and-foreign-securities

U.S. Energy Information Administration, "Europe Brent Spot Price FOB (Dollars Per Barrel)," data sourced from Thomson Reuters, release date May 19, 2021. As of May 25, 2021:
https://www.eia.gov/dnav/pet/hist/RBRTED.htm

U.S. Food and Drug Administration, "Emergency Use Authorization," webpage, last updated June 7, 2021. As of June 7, 2021:
https://www.fda.gov/emergency-preparedness-and-response/
mcm-legal-regulatory-and-policy-framework/emergency-use-authorization

U.S. Government Accountability Office, *Operation Warp Speed: Accelerated COVID-19 Vaccine Development Status and Efforts to Address Manufacturing Challenges*, Washington, D.C., GAO-21-319, February 2021.

Vanden Houten, Nancy, and Gregory Daco, "Research Briefing: Household Wealth Expands, but So Does Inequality," Oxford Economics, July 27, 2021.

Wade, Nicholas, "The Origin of COVID: Did People or Nature Open Pandora's Box at Wuhan?" *Bulletin of the Atomic Scientists*, May 5, 2021.

Wadman, Meredith, "What Does the Delta Variant Have in Store for the United States? We Asked Coronavirus Experts," *Science*, August 4, 2021.

Walker, Marcus, and Bojan Pancevski, "Troubled Covid-19 Vaccine Rollout in Europe Nears Possible Turning Point," *Wall Street Journal*, April 9, 2021.

Weiland, Noah, and Rebecca Robbins, "The U.S. Is Sitting on Tens of Millions of Vaccine Doses the World Needs," *New York Times*, March 11, 2021.

White House, *National Security Strategy of the United States*, Washington, D.C., December 2017.

———, "Fact Sheet: President Biden to Take Action on Global Health Through Support of COVAX and Calling for Health Security Financing," February 18, 2021a.

———, *Interim National Security Strategic Guidance*, Washington, D.C., March 2021b.

———, "Fact Sheet: Quad Summit," March 12, 2021c.

———, "Quad Leaders' Joint Statement: 'The Spirit of the Quad,'" Washington, D.C., March 12, 2021d.

———, "Press Briefing by White House COVID-19 Response Team and Public Health Officials," Washington, D.C., March 19, 2021e.

———, "Biden-Harris Administration Is Providing at Least 80 Million COVID-19 Vaccines for Global Use, Commits to Leading a Multilateral Effort Toward Ending the Pandemic," fact sheet, May 17, 2021f.

———, "Biden-Harris Administration Unveils Strategy for Global Vaccine Sharing, Announcing Allocation Plan for the First 25 Million Doses to Be Shared Globally," fact sheet, June 3, 2021g.

———, "United States and G7+ Plan to Defeat the COVID-19 Pandemic in 2022 and Prevent the Next Pandemic," fact sheet, June 11, 2021h.

———, *U.S. COVID-19 Global Response and Recovery Framework*, Washington, D.C., July 1, 2021i.

———, "Press Briefing by White House COVID-19 Response Team and Public Health Officials," Washington, D.C., September 2, 2021j.

White House, Office of Management and Budget, *Budget of the U.S. Government, Fiscal Year 2022*, Washington, D.C., May 28, 2021.

World Bank Group, *World Development Indicators*, database, Washington, D.C., version last updated October 15, 2020.

———, *Russia's Economic Recovery Gathers Pace: Special Focus on Cost-Effective Safety Nets*, Washington, D.C., No. 45, May 2021.

World Economic Forum, "Now Is the Time for a 'Great Reset,'" June 3, 2020.

World Health Organization, "WHO Lists Two Additional COVID-19 Vaccines for Emergency Use and COVAX Roll-Out," news release, Geneva, Switzerland, February 15, 2021a.

———, "Status of COVID-19 Vaccines Within WHO EUL/PQ Evaluation Process," guidance document, August 19, 2021b.

World Trade Organization, "Trade Falls Steeply in First Half of 2020," press release, Geneva, Switzerland, June 22, 2020a.

———, "Trade Shows Signs of Rebound from COVID-19, Recovery Still Uncertain," press release, Geneva, Switzerland, October 6, 2020b.

———, "World Trade Primed for Strong but Uneven Recovery After COVID-19 Pandemic Shock," press release, Geneva, Switzerland, March 31, 2021.

Wright, Thomas, "Biden's Misstep in India," *The Atlantic*, April 28, 2021.

Xi Jinping, "Secure a Decisive Victory in Building a Moderately Prosperous Society in All Respects and Strive for the Great Success of Socialism with Chinese Characteristics for a New Era," speech delivered at the 19th National Congress of the Communist Party of China, Beijing, October 18, 2017.

———, "Pulling Together Through Adversity and Toward a Shared Future for All," keynote speech delivered at the Boao Forum for Asia Annual Conference 2021, Boao, China, April 20, 2021.

Xie, Stella Yifan, "For China's Small Businesses, Life Is Still Far from Normal," *Wall Street Journal*, May 2, 2021a.

———, "China's Strict Covid-19 Strategy Risks Slowing Economic Recovery as Delta Variant Hits," *Wall Street Journal*, August 10, 2021b.

Zhang, Laney, "China: Health QR Code Now Required for Foreigners Flying to China," *Global Legal Monitor*, Library of Congress, December 14, 2020.